Beginning
Constitutional Law

Second edition

NICK HOWARD

Routledge
Taylor & Francis Group

LONDON AND NEW YORK

Second edition published 2017
by Routledge
2 Park Square, Milton Park, Abingdon, Oxon, OX14 4RN

and by Routledge
711 Third Avenue, New York, NY 10017

Routledge is an imprint of the Taylor & Francis Group, an informa business

First edition published 2013 by Routledge

British Library Cataloguing in Publication Data
A catalogue record for this book is available from the British Library

Library of Congress Cataloguing in Publication Data
Names: Howard, Nick, author.
Title: Beginning constitutional law / Nick Howard.
Description: Second edition. | Abingdon, Oxon; New York, NY : Routledge, 2017. |
Series: Beginning the law | Includes bibliographical references.
Identifiers: LCCN 2016002774 | ISBN 9781138189300 (hbk) | ISBN 9781138189317 (pbk)
Subjects: LCSH: Constitutional law–Great Britain.
Classification: LCC KD3989.6.H69 2017 | DDC 342.41–dc23
LC record available at http://lccn.loc.gov/2016002774

ISBN: 9781138189300 (hbk)
ISBN: 9781138189317 (pbk)
ISBN: 9781315641669 (ebk)

Typeset in Vectora LH
by Out of House Publishing

MIX
Paper from
responsible sources
FSC
www.fsc.org   FSC® C013056

Printed and bound in Great Britain by
TJ International Ltd, Padstow, Cornwall

Beginning
Constitutional Law

Whether you're new to higher education, coming to legal study for the first time or just wondering what Constitutional Law is all about, **Beginning Constitutional Law** is the ideal introduction to help you hit the ground running. Adopting a clear and simple approach with legal vocabulary explained in a detailed glossary available on the companion website, Nick Howard breaks the subject of Constitutional Law down using practical everyday examples to make it understandable for anyone, whatever their background. Diagrams and flowcharts simplify complex issues, important cases are identified and explained, and on-the-spot questions help you recognise potential issues or debates within the law so that you can contribute in classes with confidence.

This second edition has been updated to keep up to date with developments both before and after the 2015 General Election as well as ongoing proposals for reform, including:

- The referendum on independence for Scotland, increased devolved powers and the continued threat of the break-up of the Union.
- Proposals to repeal the Human Rights Act 1998 and replace it with a British Bill of Rights.
- The in/out referendum on EU membership.
- Reform of the role and composition of the House of Lords.

Beginning Constitutional Law is an ideal first introduction to the subject for LLB, GDL or ILEX and especially international students, those enrolled on distance learning courses or on other degree programmes.

Nick Howard is a Lawyer in the Office of the Counsel General for Wales and was a member of the legal Bill team who took the Government of Wales Act 2006 through Parliament. He is also a former Principal Lecturer in Constitutional Law at the University of South Wales.

Contents

Table of Cases

Table of Legislation

Preface

This book is an introduction to the UK's constitution. This is a dynamic area of law and politics – the last 20 years have seen a surge of constitutional reform. Issues such as the UK's relationship with the European Union, the relationship between the UK and its constituent nations and the balance struck between individual civil liberties and the wider public interest under the Human Rights Act 1998 continue to generate debate among politicians, the media and the public.

This book assumes no prior knowledge of the UK's constitution. It starts from scratch, examining the institutions of government and the relationships between them in clear, practical terms. It uses plain English, diagrams and realistic contemporary examples to illuminate the key topics. You can check your progress through a companion website hosting short 'pop quiz' tests and more detailed assessment-style questions and answers. It aims to help you to enjoy studying constitutional law and to pass your examination. More importantly, it encourages you to think about your own democratic rights, as lawyers, citizens and electors.

I would like to thank Fiona Briden, Emily Wells and their colleagues at Routledge for overseeing the preparation and production of this 2nd edition of the book. I am also grateful for the generous and constructive feedback from reviewers, which has helped me to improve it.

Since writing the previous edition, I have returned to practising constitutional law in the Office of the Counsel General at the Welsh Government in Cardiff. I am fortunate indeed to be working at the cutting edge of constitutional reform, in a job which is fast-moving, challenging and hugely enjoyable. My colleagues are brilliant, creative lawyers who are passionate about what they do. Working with them, I like to think, has made me a better constitutional lawyer.

I accept full responsibility for any errors or omissions in the text. The law is stated as it stood on 18 January 2016.

Nick Howard, Wales
January 2016

Guide to the Companion Website

www.routledge.com/cw/beginningthelaw

Visit the *Beginning the Law* website to discover a comprehensive range of resources designed to enhance your learning experience.

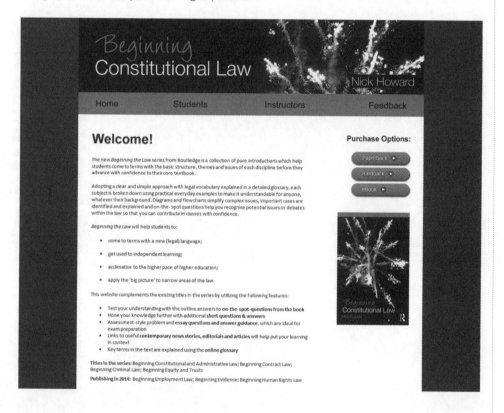

Answers to on-the-spot questions
Podcasts from the authors provide pointers and advice on how to answer the on-the-spot questions in the book.

Online Glossary
Reinforce your legal vocabulary with our online glossary flashcards. The Flashcards can be used online, or downloaded for reference on the go. Key terms are emboldened throughout the book, and you will find a deck of simple and easy to understand definitions of all of these terms for each chapter of the book here.

Case Flashcards

Test your knowledge of the key cases with this deck of Flashcards which could be used to identify either the case name from the precedent set or the precedent from the case name. The Flashcards can be used online, or downloaded for revision on the go.

Weblinks

Discover more with this set of online links to sources of further interest. These include links to contemporary news stories, editorials and articles, illuminating key issues in the text.

Updates

Twice a year, our authors provide you with updates of the latest cases, articles and debates within the law, so you can be confident you will always keep on track with the very latest developments.

Chapter 1

Introduction

WHAT IS CONSTITUTIONAL LAW?

Constitutional law is about power. It gives power to the people and institutions that make our laws, govern, police and judge us. It also sets limits to their power.

It is also about rights. The aim of this book is not just to help you to succeed in and enjoy your study of this dynamic subject, but to leave you with a better understanding of your own rights, whether as a citizen and voter, or a visitor to the United Kingdom.

Constitutional law is a fast-developing area and is constantly in the news. Issues such as the United Kingdom's membership of the European Union, decisions to go to war or take military action, the distribution of power between the United Kingdom and the nations it comprises (see below) and the question of how best to balance individual human rights with the wider public interest all engage important questions of constitutional law, and are currently right at the top of the political agenda. This means that there is a lot of debate and discussion about them on television, in newspapers and online. By watching, reading about, listening to and participating in those debates, you can breathe life and relevance into your studies, and develop a deeper understanding of the topics covered in this book.

> ### Key Definitions: United Kingdom (UK)
>
> The UK is the United Kingdom of Great Britain (an island comprising the nations of England, Wales and Scotland) and Northern Ireland.
>
> The UK is a State, i.e. a political organisation with an independent Government administering an area with internationally recognised borders.
>
> The UK comprises four different nations. England and Wales have shared a common legal system for almost 500 years, and were united with Scotland by the Act of Union 1707. The history of Northern Ireland is complex, but in effect it became part of the UK in 1922, when the rest of Ireland formed an independent State.
>
> The UK's Parliament at Westminster (in London, England) is the ultimate law-maker for all four nations, but has recently given away (or 'devolved') some of its law-making power to institutions in Wales, Scotland and Northern Ireland. We will examine this further in Chapter 6.

THE AIMS OF THIS BOOK

Lawyers need to understand the constitution, because it sets out how laws are made, changed and repealed. In that sense, it underpins all the other areas of law that you will study on your course. For that reason, constitutional law (also known as 'public law') is a compulsory subject on most law courses.

This book is an introduction to UK constitutional law. It is primarily aimed at students beginning their legal studies, whether on an undergraduate LLB degree course, a postgraduate GDL course or a combined honours course with a law element. It may also be useful to history and politics students who want to know more about our constitution. It can be read before, during and after your studies as a complement to the material delivered by your course tutor in lectures and seminars, and the more detailed texts to which they will refer you.

The book is also intended to be a useful revision aid. We will look at how you can use the material covered in each chapter to develop your understanding of the UK's constitution, and write better answers to coursework and examinations. Chapter 11 contains specific guidance on how you can draw together the topics in earlier chapters to write persuasive essays on some key contemporary issues, which are likely to crop up in examinations!

This book is more, however, than just a set of pass-notes. It is intended to interest you in the constitution and to empower you by making you more aware of your own rights, and how you can assert and enforce them. There is something of a double-whammy going on here – if you enjoy studying something and you can see its relevance, you are more likely to succeed at it!

STUDYING CONSTITUTIONAL LAW

The UK's constitution is a fascinating and fast-moving area of law – the last 20 years have seen a surge of constitutional reform. Issues such as the future of the electoral system, the accountability of Government Ministers, the sharing of power between the nations which together make up the UK and the balance struck between individual civil liberties and the wider public interest continue to generate debate among politicians, the media and the general public.

So it is surprising that little time is devoted to these issues in schools. While most students beginning a law degree have some understanding of how criminal law works and of the basic rules of contract, relatively few understand important constitutional matters such as the difference between Parliament and Government, how elections are decided and the status of their own fundamental human rights. This is not their fault – it's simply that no-one has yet explained it to them.

This book assumes no prior knowledge of the UK's constitution. It starts from the beginning, explaining what a constitution is and why States have them. It explains how and why the UK's constitution is unique, and explores the key legal principles and political dynamics underpinning the relationship between Parliament, the Government and the courts. It does so in plain English, using practical examples and illustrations, and contemporary examples to illuminate the key topics. You can check on your progress through short 'pop quiz' tests and more detailed assessment-style questions and answers on the companion website.

Beyond the book and website, it is important that, in addition to reading the material to which you are directed by your tutor, you keep up to date with the news. This does not mean that you have to turn into a recluse who just studies law and reads the newspaper from cover to cover each day! But in this subject, perhaps more than any other, the law is inseparable from the politics behind it. If you can at least keep up to date with the daily news headlines, whether via the TV, the internet, the radio or a newspaper, you will have a deeper understanding of the topics your lecturer is covering and you will ultimately find your studies more satisfying (as well as writing better, more informed essays!).

Throughout the book, you will find signposts at the end of each chapter to clear, accessible resources (many of which are freely available on the internet) which can help you to keep up to date. Chapter 11 also contains more detailed suggestions of resources which will add value to your answers to exam and coursework questions on specific topics.

While this book therefore aims to provide clear and concise guidance, to help you both to get started on your study of the constitution and to recap (both as you go along and at the end of your course) on key topics, it is not a substitute for attending classes. It is vital if you want to do well – and to enjoy your study of the law – that you go to your lectures and seminars, and that you prepare thoroughly for them. Not only will you get the benefit of your tutor's skill, knowledge and experience, but you will have the opportunity both to ask questions and to learn from your fellow students.

Most graduates, in later years, look back on University as a special time in their lives – make the most of it, give your best in class, get to know your colleagues and you will not only enjoy your studies, but you will form relationships and friendships which in many cases will last for a lifetime.

The flowchart shows how you can integrate this book with your studies. Constitutional law courses are usually structured topic-by-topic, with a lecture on each topic followed by a seminar for which you have to prepare. Examinations and coursework are often based on issues covered in seminars.

Try reading through the chapter on each topic before the relevant lecture – you will get more out of it and know what questions to ask. Then complete any directed reading given to you by your tutor and any other preparation you are asked to do for the seminar. Participate in the seminar as much as you can, and use the opportunity to seek clarification on any issues which you are finding difficult. Do not be frightened to ask! Other students are, more than likely, struggling with the same points, and your tutor will be only too happy to answer – we do actually like being asked questions!

After the seminar, re-read the chapter to consolidate your knowledge and understanding, then attempt the follow-up exercises on the companion website. Doing this now, rather than waiting until after the course ends, will help the key points to sink in and make your revision easier when it comes to the exam period – honestly!

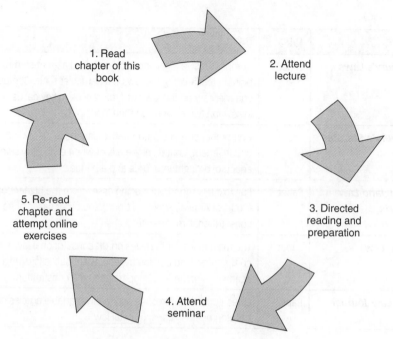

Figure 1.1   Route map to successful study

FINDING CONSTITUTIONAL LAW

As you will see in Chapter 3, the UK's constitution is found in a variety of sources. While this book, and your tutor, will direct you to and summarise the key cases and legislation, as your studies progress, you will need to access these yourself. In particular, any coursework element to your assessment is likely to require you to carry out detailed, independent legal research.

When you start your course, you will be shown how to use and access various online and paper resources which are essential to your legal studies. Some of the key ones (and those most widely used by practising lawyers) are:

Source	Type	Use
LexisLibrary	Online	Comprehensive, up-to-date database of all current legislation, with full text law reports of key cases.
Westlaw	Online	As above, with a useful index of legal journals (see below).
Lawtel	Online	Up-to-date legislation and case law, with a useful e-notification feature to alert you to new cases and Bills.

(*Continued*)

Source	Type	Use
Halsbury's Laws	Paper	Comprehensive legal encyclopaedia and a great starting point in researching the law on a particular topic. Contains commentary on the law, with references to key cases and legislation (which you can then look up).
Halsbury's Statutes	Paper	Comprehensive and authoritative paper source of UK Acts of Parliament, containing details of when each provision was enacted, brought into force and amended.
All England Law Reports	Paper	Full text law reports of leading cases from the higher courts (Court of Appeal, Supreme Court) and other cases of general constitutional importance.
Public Law	Paper	The main journal for articles on UK constitutional law, with commentary and opinion by leading UK public law judges and academics on new developments in the constitution.
New Law Journal	Paper	Often contains interesting and highly readable articles on new developments in constitutional law.

Please note that this is not a comprehensive list! There are many good alternative sources available. Make use of any opportunities afforded by your University library, your course induction programme or publishers' representatives and student ambassadors to familiarise yourself with the law content of both the paper library and the online resources available to you.

PRIMARY AND SECONDARY SOURCES

It is important that you are able to distinguish between primary and secondary sources in your research.

Primary sources are the law itself – case law, Acts of Parliament and regulations made under them (see more about this in Chapter 3).

Secondary sources include text books, encyclopaediae (such as *Halsbury's Laws*), volumes of statutes and law reports (such as *Halsbury's Statutes* or the *All England Law Reports*) and periodical journals (such as *Public Law*). These resources are not, themselves, the law – but they will help you to find it and to understand it.

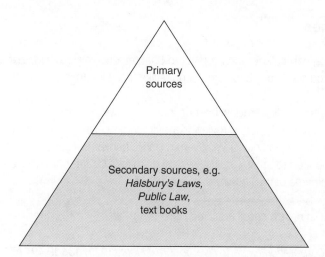

It is essential, when putting together a legal argument (whether in a real-life court case, a student essay or an answer to a seminar question!), that it is based on primary sources, i.e. case law and legislation which relates to the topic under discussion and supports your point. You can use secondary sources as a launch pad to help you to find the key primary sources – e.g. by looking up a topic in the index to a text book on constitutional law and then seeing which cases and legislation the author's commentary on the topic refers to. Take a note of the details (for legislation, the Act's name and year, and the section number; for case law, the full citation). It will then be much easier to find the primary source than if you were to go straight online.

For example, if you go onto Westlaw and search for cases about judicial review (see Chapter 8), it returns over 4,000 cases! Work smarter, not harder – think of legal research as a bit like climbing a mountain and use secondary sources as a base camp from which you can reach the primary sources at the peak.

TERMINOLOGY

When you are new to a subject, it is easy to become confused and put off by jargon. While this book uses plain English, there are some key terms which all constitutional lawyers and students need to know and use, and which may at first be alien to you.

Do not worry – this book is supported by a glossary which offers simple explanations of the terms highlighted in bold throughout the text. You may find it helpful both to read through the glossary before you start the book and to keep it flagged with a bookmark or Post-it, so that you can turn to it as and when you need to.

Key legislation and case law is also highlighted in bold.

Case names

You may notice, particularly when you get to Chapter 8 (judicial review), that some of the case names you see in this book are not quite like those in other areas of the law.

You will read about judicial review later on, but at this stage it may be helpful to explain how the cases are cited. Judicial review is a civil law process by which citizens challenge the legality of actions and decisions taken by public bodies. Because the permission of the court is required to bring a judicial review claim (see Chapter 8), cases are cited as if brought in the name of the Crown.

Pre-2001, judicial review cases are cited like this:

R v Liverpool Corporation ex parte Liverpool Taxi Fleet (1972) 136 JP 491

'*R*' stands for '*Regina*', which is Latin for 'Queen', and reflects the fact that cases are brought in the name of the Crown. '*Ex parte*' (sometimes abbreviated to '*ex p*') is Latin and means 'on behalf of'. What this citation tells us is that this is a judicial review case, brought against Liverpool Corporation (a public body, the defendant) by Liverpool Taxi Fleet (the claimant). It was reported in 1972, in the 136th volume of the *Justice of the Peace Reports*, at page 491.

After 2001, as part of a general move to rid UK law of unnecessary Latin, the method of citing judicial review cases changed. Case citations now look like this:

R (Daly) v Secretary of State for the Home Department [2001] AC 532

Cases are still brought in the name of the Crown, but the claimant's name (here, Daly) is placed in brackets afterwards, with the identity of the defendant (here, the Home Secretary) following the '*v*', which stands for '*versus*', meaning 'against' (so they have not quite got rid of all the Latin!). So this is Daly's claim for judicial review of a decision made by the Home Secretary, reported in 2001 at page 532 of the *Law Reports, Appeal Cases* volume for that year.

Both of these cases will be discussed in detail in Chapter 8.

WHAT APPROACH DOES THIS BOOK TAKE?

As you will see, the UK's constitution is far from being neat and tidy! Different books, and different lecturers, approach the constitution in different ways. There are certain key topics, however, that all constitutional law courses cover – these include the institutions of the State (Parliament, Government and the judiciary), their personnel and powers, the dynamics of the relationships between them and the impact upon all of the above of the Human Rights Act 1998.

This book begins by asking what is a constitution and why do States have them? We will introduce you to the UK's constitution, explaining how and why it differs fundamentally from that of almost every other State – in particular, we will compare it to the United States of America's Constitution (Chapter 2).

We will then look at the different sources of UK constitutional law (Chapter 3) and the underlying principles on which the rules of the constitution are based (Chapter 4).

If you had to describe the UK's constitution in three words, you might describe it as 'a Parliamentary democracy'. In Chapters 5, 6 and 7 we will examine the make-up and functions of Parliament, its law-making powers and its relationship with Government.

Government's personnel and powers, and its relationship with the courts, are examined in detail in Chapter 8. Its relationship with individuals is examined in Chapter 9, where we consider the impact of the Human Rights Act 1998 upon those who govern us, and the key provisions of the European Convention on Human Rights which that Act incorporated into domestic law. In Chapter 10, we consider Convention rights further, in the specific context of police powers of arrest and powers to restrict civil liberties, such as the right to protest.

You will find that some topics, such as the Human Rights Act 1998, non-legal conventions, the rule of law and the separation of powers, crop up in several chapters. Because (as you can see from the diagram at the end of this chapter!) the UK's constitution is not neatly compartmentalised, some overlap between topics (and therefore chapters) is inevitable. But this is not mere repetition – the aim of the book is to encourage you to revisit and reflect on ideas and theories introduced in the earlier chapters, as you develop your knowledge of the key institutions and their powers through subsequent reading. On-the-spot questions throughout the text encourage you to make links between the topics you study, so that you build up layers of understanding about the constitution with each successive chapter.

In Chapter 11, we draw together the theories and the detailed law we have studied into model answer plans to three topics of contemporary relevance. While these are not the only topics on which you may be asked exam questions, the aim is to show you how to revise effectively and marshal your information into concise, authoritative, persuasive and interesting essays – a skill which will serve you well not just in this subject, but in any area of legal study!

SUMMARY

- Constitutional law is a dynamic and engaging area of the law, which empowers and regulates those who govern us, while providing citizens with key civil liberties and voting rights.
- The UK's constitution is not neat and tidy, but by using this book to prepare for and recap upon your attendance at lectures and seminars, you can develop a coherent, structured approach to study. The diagram overleaf gives you an overview of the institutions of the constitution and the chapters in which they are examined.
- Keep up to date with the news, using the resources highlighted in this book and by your tutor to add colour and life to your studies by relating the topics you are studying to current political events.
- Use the online resources which accompany the book to check your knowledge and understanding as you go along, and to help you to prepare for seminars and to revise for examinations.
- Enjoy your studies! Use what you have learnt in this book to empower you, both as a lawyer and as a citizen – the rights discussed in this book are your rights.

Note: at the end of each chapter of this book, some further reading is suggested to help you to consolidate and extend your knowledge of each topic. This usually comprises three different sources – often a text book, a journal or newspaper article and an online blog or report. These are not exhaustive: as noted above, there are lots of reliable and stimulating secondary sources available on constitutional law. But they have been chosen because they are accessible, contemporary and thought-provoking – we hope that you enjoy reading them!

The UK constitution at a glance

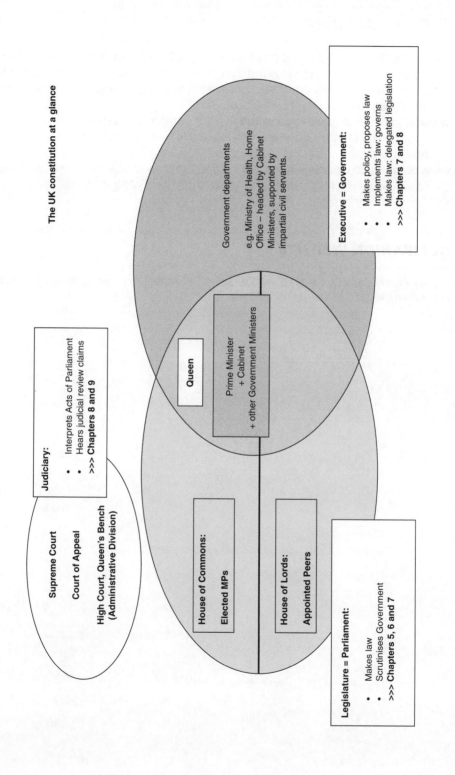

Judiciary:

- Interprets Acts of Parliament
- Hears judicial review claims

>>> **Chapters 8 and 9**

Supreme Court

Court of Appeal

High Court, Queen's Bench
(Administrative Division)

Queen

Prime Minister
+ Cabinet
+ other Government Ministers

Government departments

e.g. Ministry of Health, Home
Office – headed by Cabinet
Ministers, supported by
impartial civil servants.

Executive = Government:

- Makes policy, proposes law
- Implements law: governs
- Makes law: delegated legislation

>>> **Chapters 7 and 8**

House of Commons:

Elected MPs

House of Lords:

Appointed Peers

Legislature = Parliament:

- Makes law
- Scrutinises Government

>>> **Chapters 5, 6 and 7**

FURTHER READING

Jowell, J and Oliver, D, *The Changing Constitution*, 8th edn, 2015, Oxford: Oxford University Press – a collection of concise, scholarly and thought-provoking essays on various aspects of the constitution and recent or potential reforms. Perhaps best tackled once you are more familiar with the key topics as outlined in this book.

www.guardian.co.uk/politics/constitution – *The Guardian* newspaper's online home page on constitutional reform. Worth checking regularly to keep up to date with political and legal developments.

www.ucl.ac.uk/constitution-unit – an influential think-tank based at University College London whose website contains links to research and blogs about the constitution.

COMPANION WEBSITE

An online glossary compiled by the author is available on the companion website: www.routledge.com/cw/beginningthelaw

Chapter 2

Does the UK have a constitution?

LEARNING OBJECTIVES

After reading this chapter, you should be able to:

- Define and explain the purpose of a constitution
- Understand the concepts of the rule of law and the separation of powers
- Describe a constitution by identifying its key features
- Compare the UK's constitution to that of the USA
- Explain why the UK's constitution is unique.

INTRODUCTION

The question 'does the UK have a constitution?' is an important one, because it is the constitution of a State that sets out:

- the key rights of its citizens;
- how and by whom the State is to be governed;
- limits on the power of the Government.

So it is to the constitution that a State's citizens turn to find the answers to important questions about their own rights and about the legality of Government action.

Most States have a **codified constitution**, i.e. a single document in which the most important rules of the constitution are set out. The UK does not have a codified constitution, but it does have laws and other non-legal rules establishing citizens' rights, mechanisms for Government and limits on Government power.

Some people in the UK think that it is time that those rules were codified into a single, authoritative legal document so that everyone knows where to find the rules and what they are. Others think that an uncodified constitution is 'unnecessary, undesirable and un-British'.[1] They prefer the flexibility that an uncodified constitution offers and say, 'if the system isn't broken, there is no need to fix it'.

---

[1] *A New Magna Carta?*, House of Commons Political and Constitutional Reform Committee, Second Report of Session 2014–15, 3 July 2014.

This chapter will:

- explain in more detail what a constitution is; and why States have them;
- introduce you to the **rule of law** and the doctrine of the **separation of powers**, two key principles underlying constitutional theory;
- examine the codified Constitution of the United States of America (USA), so that you can compare and contrast this with the UK's uncodified constitution;
- explain how and why the UK's constitution is different from that of other States; and
- at the end, invite you to start forming your own view about whether the UK should have a codified constitution, and to keep revisiting and developing that view as you read through the rest of this book.

This chapter will explain how and why the UK's constitution is different from that of other countries. It will introduce you to some key principles of constitutional law, such as the separation of powers and the rule of law. It will also examine the Constitution of the USA so that when you come to write essays on this topic, you can compare and contrast the USA's codified constitution with the UK's less formal arrangements.

WHAT IS A CONSTITUTION?

Any organisation can have a constitution. At a national or 'state' level, a constitution may be defined as:

Key Definition

Constitution: 'the whole system of government of a country, the collection of rules which establish and regulate or govern the government'.

Sir Kenneth Wheare, *Modern Constitutions* (1965)

WHY HAVE A CONSTITUTION?

A **constitution** is a body of rules that sets out how an organisation is run, who runs it and what powers they have to do so. Any organisation, from a small private members' club to the **European Union**, can have a constitution.

For example, I play for a local cricket team. At the end of last season, after a narrow defeat in the cup final, our captain resigned. Several players (including the club secretary) were keen to take over from him. This raised a number of questions. How would we decide on the new captain – was this a decision to be taken by the committee members who run the club or by all of its players? Which players were eligible to stand? If the club secretary took over as captain, could he do both jobs?

To resolve these issues, we turned to the club's constitution. All the answers were there. The club secretary had to call a meeting. Each player was entitled to attend and vote on who should be captain. Any player was eligible to stand for election and was entitled to make a brief speech at the meeting outlining their credentials. The club secretary would have to resign his current post if elected as captain, because the constitution does not allow the same person to do both jobs. Why not? Because the club's constitution requires both the captain and the secretary to agree on matters such as team selection. If one person did both jobs, they would have total control over the team.

Perhaps all this sounds a little formal. But when the club was set up a few years ago, the original members wanted it to be run fairly, openly and in the best interests of its members. They did not want a few senior players taking all the decisions to the exclusion of everyone else. This would be unsustainable – after a while, the other players would become dissatisfied. The constitution is only a short document, but it is easy to read and it is published on the club's website.[2] Everyone can see how the club's committee members are chosen, what powers they have to spend the players' membership fees and how the players can remove them if they feel they are underperforming.

So my cricket team may not be cup winners, but we are a **democracy** – a society (albeit a very small one!) in which the power to govern derives from, exists subject to the consent of and is regulated by the people being governed. The constitution plays an important role within that democracy because it enables the players to understand, get involved with and take ownership of the running of their club.

You might think that if an amateur cricket club would go to the trouble of having a constitution, then so would an organisation as important, powerful and wealthy as a national **Government**. And, indeed, almost every country in the world has (like my cricket team) what is known as a **codified constitution** – a single document which establishes the institutions which run that country, sets out their powers and protects the key rights

---

[2] www.glamorgancenturions.co.uk/constitution.html.

and civil liberties of its citizens. The only three countries in the world which do not have this kind of constitution are Israel, New Zealand and… the **UK**.

THE UK'S CONSTITUTION

By Sir Kenneth Wheare's definition, the UK has a constitution. Like other countries, it has a body of rules which establish and regulate the Government. For example, it has rules about how elections to the **House of Commons** are contested and how a Government is formed following such an election. It has laws which confer duties, powers and functions on the Government, and also laws which (to some extent) limit the Government's power to interfere with individuals' civil liberties. It has a legal system, which allows citizens to challenge the Government in the courts where they allege that their rights have been unlawfully infringed. We will examine the most important of these rules in detail later on in this book.

What is unusual about the UK's constitution, however, is that it is uncodified. In other words, the rules of our constitution have not been organised into a single, easily accessible document. Some of them are not even written down at all and cannot be enforced in the courts. For example, you might be surprised to learn that there is no clear rule as to how the **Prime Minister** is chosen following a General Election. Legally, the **Queen** is free to appoint whoever she likes as Prime Minister. In reality, an unwritten rule (or **convention**) has developed under which the Queen usually appoints as Prime Minister the leader of the political party which has a majority of Members of Parliament (MPs) in the House of Commons. The UK's uncodified constitution is therefore a curious mixture of written laws (which can be enforced in the courts) and unwritten conventions (which cannot). Even those rules of our constitution which are written down and are legally enforceable, such as the **Human Rights Act 1998**, have no special status which marks them out as being any more important than other, relatively trivial, laws, such as the **Sunbeds (Regulation) Act 2010**, although as we will see in Chapter 6, there are some signs that this is beginning to change.

To understand how the UK's constitution has evolved in this way, we need to compare and contrast it with the codified constitutions of other countries. Why did they do something different?

WHY DO OTHER STATES HAVE CODIFIED CONSTITUTIONS?

Most other countries around the world have adopted a codified constitution as a result of cataclysmic events such as a military defeat, a political crisis, a popular revolution or a declaration of independence from a former colonial power. Examples include:

Country	Date	Reason for adopting a codified constitution
USA	1787	America's declaration of independence from Britain, its former colonial ruler, and the consequent need to create a new system of Government which would be fair, just and protective of its citizens.
France	1791	The French Revolution, a popular revolt against the monarchy caused by widespread poverty, hunger and malnutrition, which led to the storming of the Bastille, in which guns and ammunition were stored.
	1958	Collapse of the French Fourth Republic, following the Algerian War, military revolt and the failure of the French Parliament to choose a Government led to France adopting a new constitution.
Germany	1949	Defeat in World War II and a desire to avoid a system which could result in the totalitarian style of Government which characterised Nazi rule during the Third Reich.
Russia	1993	A national economic crisis and credit crunch led to a political conflict between the President and the Parliament, which ended in the dissolution and storming of the Russian Parliament.

How does the adoption of a codified constitution help countries to respond to events such as these? The answer is that such a constitution marks a new start for the country, both legally and politically. Legally, it establishes and populates the key institutions without which the country cannot function, i.e. the Government, the law-making body and the courts. It also defines the boundaries of those institutions' power. This is important to prevent a repetition of the kind of tyranny which sparked the events which led to the drafting of a new constitution – e.g. the abuses of power by King Louis XVI in eighteenth-century France or by Adolf Hitler in twentieth-century Germany. The constitution gives the people a legal mechanism with which to restrain, and ultimately remove, their leaders.

Usually, a codified constitution embodies certain 'higher laws' which are elevated above other 'ordinary laws' in that country's legal system. It does this by making those 'higher laws' or 'constitutional laws' more difficult to change or get rid of ('repeal') than ordinary laws. For example, the constitution itself may say that it can only be changed with the consent of the people of that country, as signified by a vote in a **referendum**. Or it may say that a special majority of the people's elected representatives in the law-making body is required in order to change it. This protection of the higher laws set out in the constitution is called **entrenchment**.

Typically, the constitution establishes a special Supreme Court, or Constitutional Court, to police and enforce these higher laws. Consider this example from Germany:

KEY CASE: *Bundesverfassungsgericht*, 1 BvR 357/05, 15 February 2006

Background:

The German law-making bodies passed the Aviation Security Act 2005. The Act allowed the German armed forces to shoot down hijacked civilian airliners over Germany in the event of a terrorist attack. The purpose of this was to prevent hijacked airliners being deliberately flown into buildings, as had happened with the destruction of the World Trade Center in the USA on 9/11.

Principle:

The German Constitutional Court declared the Act to be incompatible with German Basic Law under the constitution. This was because it violated:

- the prohibition on German military action within Germany's borders; and
- the fundamental right to life of civilian passengers and the guarantee of their human dignity.

The Act was therefore invalid.

On-the-spot question

What if the UK Parliament passed an Act allowing the Royal Air Force to shoot down hijacked civilian airliners – should the UK Supreme Court have the power to strike that Act down? Or is this the sort of difficult decision we elect and trust our MPs to take?

By choosing to entrench and prioritise certain laws in the way that Germany has done, the people adopting a codified constitution are making a significant statement about the values they prize most highly – for example, the right to human dignity, the right to free speech or the right to freedom of religious worship. In doing so, the constitution becomes an important symbol of national, cultural identity, which is taught about in schools and which high-ranking officials (such as the President of the USA) must swear to uphold. So a codified constitution is more than just a legal document. It has a significant political value too.

The idea that a codified constitution is a document of both legal and political importance reflects an important constitutional theory which you need to understand to write essays about this subject – the **rule of law**.

THE RULE OF LAW

The rule of law is a notoriously difficult concept to pin down. There has been much discussion among academics, lawyers and political scientists about precisely what it means. It is capable of both a narrow definition and a wide definition.

At its simplest, the rule of law involves three propositions, as set out by A V Dicey in his book *An Introduction to the Study of the Law of the Constitution* (1885). The language used by Dicey is complex and old-fashioned, but a plain English version of his definition of the rule of law essentially boils down to three principles:

1. Nobody can be punished unless they are proved in court to have broken a law.
2. Nobody is above the law – the courts treat everyone equally.
3. The courts will provide a remedy for any breach of an individual's legal rights.

Although Dicey was writing well over 100 years ago, his ideas about the constitution are still very influential on judges, politicians and constitutional law lecturers – including, in all likelihood, the person setting your exam paper!

Dicey's 'thin' definition of the rule of law has been criticised for being too narrow. While it emphasises the importance of formality, certainty and equality in the law, it does not acknowledge that a corrupt State could oppress its people using laws which are evil and unfair. So long as the courts uphold and apply such laws uniformly, the Government could argue that it is complying with the rule of law. Dictatorial regimes, such as the Nazi regime in Germany during World War II, have subverted the concept of the rule of law by passing laws to authorise mass murder, torture and the oppression of ethnic minorities. Such acts are no longer 'crimes' if authorised by law.

This offends common sense and most people's understanding of what a 'crime' really is. Critics such as the American constitutional lawyer Ronald Dworkin have therefore argued that the rule of law demands more than just a set of clearly defined and consistently applied rules. It requires the rules themselves to be fair, just and based on the common values of the people whom they govern. Otherwise, they will be considered invalid and will not be obeyed.

This much broader, 'thick' definition of the rule of law makes the validity of law dependent upon its substance or quality, and not just the process by which it is enacted. As you will see in Chapter 6 when we consider **Parliamentary sovereignty**, the UK's courts have traditionally ruled upon the validity of Parliamentary law on the basis of process rather than substance. There are signs, however, that this is beginning to change:

> ### Key Definition
>
> **Rule of law:** 'The efficacy and maintenance of the rule of law, which is the foundation of any parliamentary democracy, has at least two pre-requisites. First, people must understand that it is in their interests, as well as in that of the community as a whole, that they should live their lives in accordance with the rules and all the rules. Secondly, they must know what those rules are.'
>
> Lord Donaldson MR, *Merkur Island Shipping Co v Laughton*
> [1983] 2 AC 570

The wider concept of the rule of law fits with the idea of a codified constitution (like Germany's) articulating a form of 'higher law'; a set of shared community values which the people adopting the constitution wish to promote and protect, and against which they wish all other laws to be measured. The UK constitution, which is uncodified, does not make this distinction. It does, however, conform to Dicey's narrower definition, in which the Government is subject to the law, and is to that extent controlled by the courts. For this control to be effective, it is essential that the courts themselves are independent of Government. This leads us to another key constitutional theory – the **separation of powers**.

SEPARATION OF POWERS

> ### Key Definition
>
> **Separation of powers:** 'when the legislative and executive powers are united in the same person or the same body... there can be no liberty. Again there is no liberty if the power of judging is not separated from the legislative and the executive'.
>
> Montesquieu, *L'Esprit des Lois* (*The Spirit of the Laws*), 1748

The separation of powers is a model of Government that many countries, such as the USA, have chosen to adopt in a codified constitution. The theory has its origins in the Classical world of Ancient Greece and Rome, but was popularised in the eighteenth century by the French political philosopher, **Baron de Montesquieu.**

Montesquieu was concerned that the French monarchy had too much power. Along with other contemporary philosophers such as John Locke, he thought that if too much power was concentrated in one pair of hands, this would lead to the corruption of Government and the oppression of citizens – or 'tyranny'.

To prevent this, Montesquieu advocated a model in which the power to run the State was divided equally between three separate institutions, each performing their own independent functions, and exercising checks and balances over each other. The three branches of the State that he identified, together with a summary and examples of their functions, are set out below:

Branch	Function	Example
Legislature (i.e. in the UK, Parliament)	Makes law, giving powers to the executive to run the State	Parliament enacts the Terrorism Act 2000, giving the Government the power to 'proscribe' (ban) terrorist groups
Executive (Government)	Governs the State, using the legal powers granted by the legislature	The Government produces a list of proscribed groups whom it believes to be involved in terrorism
Judiciary (Courts)	Interprets and applies the law, restraining the executive where it goes beyond its legal powers	A group seeks a judicial review of the Government's proscription of them, on the grounds that they claim not to be involved in terrorism

In its purest form, Montesquieu's theory requires that the legislature, the executive and the judiciary are entirely separate from each other in terms of both personnel and function. In other words, nobody can work in more than one branch at a time, and no branch can carry out the function of another. Crucially, Montesquieu thought that no one branch of the State should have more power than the others. This way, each institution could act as a check on the others, e.g. if the executive acted unlawfully, the courts could restrain it, or if the legislature passed unjust laws, the executive could refuse to implement them.

It is one of the great ironies of constitutional law that Montesquieu's theory is in fact based on a misunderstanding of the UK's constitution. As you will see in the following chapters, while recent reforms have secured the structural independence of the judiciary, there is a considerable overlap of both personnel and function between Parliament (the UK's legislature, in particular the House of Commons), and Government (the executive). The UK's constitution exhibits a fusion, not a separation, of powers.

Nevertheless, even though it is based on a mistaken assumption about the UK's structure of Government, Montesquieu's theory has proved hugely influential on the authors of constitutions around the world. In particular, it forms the basis for the Constitution of the USA, which we will now examine in detail.

THE USA'S CONSTITUTION

If you are studying law in the UK, what is the point of discussing the USA's Constitution?

The answer is that to describe anything, you have to distinguish it from something else. You do this every day by using adjectives to identify the particular features which mark out the object of your discussion, e.g. the 'big, black dog', as opposed to the other, smaller, different coloured dogs (or other animals!). This technique works for constitutional law essays too. Understanding the basics of how the USA's codified Constitution operates will help you to describe the UK's uncodified constitution, as it will enable you to compare and contrast the two systems.

Republican or monarchical?

The USA has a republican Constitution in which power ultimately derives from the people, subject to whose support and consent the elected officials govern. The preamble to the Constitution reads like a modern-day mission statement:

> We the People of the United States, in Order to form a more perfect Union, establish Justice, insure domestic Tranquility, provide for the common defence, promote the general Welfare, and secure the Blessings of Liberty to ourselves and our Posterity, do ordain and establish this Constitution for the United States of America.
>
> Preamble, Constitution of the United States of America (1787)

This makes it clear that the USA's Constitution was created by the people, for the people, who are the ultimate source of legitimacy for Government action. The USA's Head of State (its chief public representative and executive officer) is the President, who is elected by the people in accordance with Article 2 of the Constitution.

By contrast, the UK is a **constitutional monarchy**. The Head of State is the Queen, who inherits her position by birth rather than through democratic elections. As you will see in Chapter 4, the Queen's constitutional role is now largely ceremonial. While the Queen remains an important symbol of continuity and national identity, real political power is exercised on her behalf by Government Ministers whom she appoints in accordance with conventions, which respect the wishes of the electorate.

Separation or fusion of powers?

The USA's Constitution is the framework for the organisation of the law-making body, the Government and the courts. This structure is clearly and deliberately based on Montesquieu's theory of the separation of powers, as shown opposite.

By contrast, as you will see in Chapters 4 and 7, there is a fusion of the legislature and the executive in the UK's constitution, with the key officials in Government being drawn from (and exercising great influence in) the House of Commons, the most powerful part of the UK's legislature.

Federal or unitary?

In addition to defining clear boundaries of power between Congress, the President and the Supreme Court, the USA's Constitution also sets out how these central, national institutions relate to the 50 individual States (e.g. California, Florida and Texas) which together in union comprise the USA. Article 4 obliges the central institutions to guarantee each individual state their own publicly elected State Government and protection against invasion. In return, Article 6 requires local law-makers, Government officials and judges in each state to swear to uphold the USA's Constitution, and to recognise it (and any laws made under it by Congress) as the supreme law of the land.

This is what is known as a **federal** constitution, i.e. one in which a union of individual states recognises the supremacy of a central authority, while retaining some powers of local self-government. The laws set out in the Constitution (such as the abolition of slavery) apply throughout the USA and cannot be changed or modified at state level. On matters in relation to which the Constitution is silent, individual states are free to legislate as they wish – for example, capital punishment (the death penalty), which is currently legal in 31 of the 50 states, but not, for example, in Iowa, New Jersey or Vermont.

By contrast, the UK's constitution has traditionally been described as a **unitary** constitution, i.e. one in which power is concentrated in one central authority, and local government exists only to the extent that central government chooses to allow. The defining feature of the UK's uncodified constitution is **Parliamentary supremacy**, which we will discuss in Chapter 6. While **devolution** (the transfer of limited law-making and executive powers to Scotland, Wales and Northern Ireland) has, to some extent, made the UK's constitution more federal, the Acts of devolution state that those powers could be reclaimed by the UK Parliament – although, as we will discuss later on in this book, it is questionable whether that is realistic.

The USA's rigid Constitution

Another key feature of the USA's codified Constitution is that it is **entrenched**. In other words, there is a special procedure for amending the law of the Constitution. This procedure is set out in the Constitution itself and is more rigorous than the procedure for making and changing ordinary American laws. In order to take effect, a proposal to amend the Constitution must be approved by:

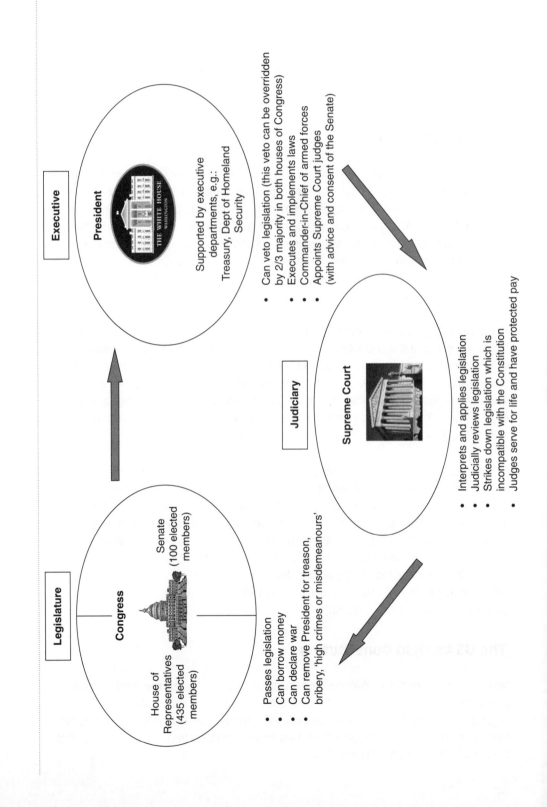

Legislature

Congress

House of Representatives (435 elected members)

Senate (100 elected members)

- Passes legislation
- Can borrow money
- Can declare war
- Can remove President for treason, bribery, 'high crimes or misdemeanours'

Executive

President

THE WHITE HOUSE
WASHINGTON

Supported by executive departments, e.g.: Treasury, Dept of Homeland Security

- Can veto legislation (this veto can be overridden by 2/3 majority in both houses of Congress)
- Executes and implements laws
- Commander-in-Chief of armed forces
- Appoints Supreme Court judges (with advice and consent of the Senate)

Judiciary

Supreme Court

- Interprets and applies legislation
- Judicially reviews legislation
- Strikes down legislation which is incompatible with the Constitution
- Judges serve for life and have protected pay

- two-thirds of the House of Representatives;
- two-thirds of the Senate; and
- three-quarters of the 50 States.

It is not impossible to achieve this. The USA's Constitution has been amended 27 times. But it is very difficult to secure the support of the special majorities to amend it. This is because the USA is, essentially, a two-party state, dominated by the Democratic and Republican Parties.

Neither of the two parties holds a two-thirds majority in either House. Nor are they likely to do so for the foreseeable future. This means that in order to change the Constitution, both of the main parties would have to agree to the proposed amendment. Since the parties politically define themselves by opposing each other, it is rare for them to agree. Even if they do, the amendment then has to be approved (or 'ratified') by three-quarters of the 50 States. As an illustration of how difficult it is to obtain their support, the most recent amendment to the USA's Constitution (Amendment 27 – limiting changes to congressional pay) was originally proposed on 25 September 1789, but was not ratified by the required number of States until 7 May 1992. The process took 203 years!

Clearly, the USA has a rigid Constitution. Is this a good thing or a bad thing? It depends on your perspective. By requiring cross-party support for amendments, the Constitution ensures that key citizens' rights such as the entitlement to trial by jury cannot easily be compromised or removed.

On-the-spot question

 Do you think that the right to a jury trial is important? Why might politicians want to get rid of it in some cases? How easy would it be for them to do so in the UK? Should the right to jury trials be protected, as in the USA?

A codified, entrenched constitution can therefore afford significant and sustained protection to those rights which it considers to be fundamental. Society may change, politicians come and go, and ordinary laws will change to reflect this. The essential rights enshrined in the constitution will endure, providing citizens with a minimum standard of human freedom and dignity which can only be changed with the approval of an overwhelming majority of the people's elected representatives.

There are, however, potential disadvantages to having such a rigid constitution. The 2nd Amendment to the USA's Constitution, ratified in 1791, provides:

> A well regulated Militia, being necessary to the security of a free State, the right of the people to keep and bear Arms, shall not be infringed.
>
> 2nd Amendment, Constitution of the United States of America (1791)

This is a very controversial provision, because it gives every citizen of the USA the absolute right to keep firearms. The pro-gun lobby, including the powerful National Rifle Association (with nearly 4 million members), defend the 2nd Amendment as a key bulwark of personal freedom, enabling citizens to defend themselves not only against each other, but potentially against an over-intrusive Government. However, following a succession of mass shootings such as the Columbine High School, Virginia Tech and San Bernardino massacres, those who favour the introduction of tighter gun controls argue that the conditions of relative political and military instability which justified its ratification in 1791 no longer apply. They claim that the provision is no longer necessary or appropriate, and that by allowing anyone and everyone to own a gun, it actually threatens rather than protects citizens' safety.

The 2nd Amendment polarises popular opinion in the USA[3], but even with polls showing that a majority of Americans favour changing gun control laws, the constitutional dice are loaded against those who wish to remove this clause. The right to own guns is so entrenched, both legally (as detailed above) and culturally (as a defining constitutional symbol of American freedom), that there is insufficient political consensus to remove it.

The UK's flexible constitution

In the UK, the right to own and keep handguns was abolished by the Firearms (Amendment) Act 1997. This Act was passed in response to the Dunblane Primary School massacre, in which 16 Primary One pupils and their teacher were shot dead using legally owned firearms. The tragedy happened in March 1996. By February 1997,[4] Parliament had legislated to ban handguns. No special majority was required to do so. The Act was passed using the same procedure as any other.

Was this a change to the UK's constitution? It is difficult to say. Parliament is the supreme law-maker in the UK and is not established or limited by any codified constitution. Accordingly, our Parliament is free to legislate as it wishes.[5] Parliament itself makes no distinction between the status of Acts as diverse as the **Constitutional Reform and Governance Act 2010**, the Protection of Badgers Act 1992 and the Football Spectators Act 1989. They are all made the same way, and it is no more difficult to change or repeal any one of them than the others. While some Acts, such as the **Human Rights Act 1998**, are considered by the judges to be

---

[3] For a further explanation of why the views of Americans expressed in recent polls are not replicated in Congress, see the BBC news article 'Why Obama is powerless to reform gun laws' (4 October 2015) at www.bbc.co.uk/news/world-us-canada-34429918.

[4] Further legislation extending the ban to high calibre handguns, the Firearms (Amendment) (No 2) Act 1997, was passed in November 1997.

[5] Though it is argued that Parliament can, and has, limited its own legislative competence – see Chapter 6.

'constitutional statutes',[6] they can (as you will see in Chapter 5) be repealed by, in effect, just one more MP voting to get rid of them than to keep them.

WHY IS THE UK'S CONSTITUTION SO DIFFERENT FROM THE USA'S?

We noted earlier in this chapter that most codified constitutions are adopted in response to some watershed, nation-defining event such as revolution, invasion or (as in the USA's case) a declaration of independence.

The reason that the UK does not have a codified constitution is principally because it has not experienced this kind of political or military 'big bang' in almost 1,000 years since the Norman Conquest. While there has been significant constitutional change (such as the gradual transfer of power from the monarchy to Parliament and the widening of the electoral franchise), this has happened incrementally, step-by-step, rather than in one fell swoop. Compared with the revolutionary fervour that swept other European countries in the eighteenth and nineteenth centuries, the UK's political history has been remarkably stable. Is this because of, or in spite of, our uncodified, flexible constitution?

SUMMARY

- The USA's Constitution is the classic example of a codified constitution, based on the separation of powers. It is a republican, federal constitution which entrenches key civil liberties against change or repeal.
- The UK's constitutional monarchy is uncodified, unitary and flexible. While this allows the law to respond quickly to events such as the Dunblane massacre, it does leave citizens' fundamental rights vulnerable to change.
- As yet, there has not been a sufficient political impetus to codify the disparate rules of the UK's constitution into a single, organised legal document. Towards the end of this book, when you know more about what those rules are and how they have developed, we will ask whether the time is now right to do so.

---

[6] See the discussion of the *Thoburn* (2002) and *H v Lord Advocate* (2013) cases in Chapter 6.

ISSUES TO THINK ABOUT FURTHER

As you read each chapter of this book, you should reflect on the UK's uncodified constitution and consider whether – as a citizen, a voter and a lawyer – you are happy with the level of protection it affords your rights.

Do you trust the UK's constitutional monarchy, and the politicians whom our electoral system returns, to look after your interests?

Or do you think that our constitution should be more like the USA's? What would be the advantages and disadvantages of having a codified, entrenched constitution?

FURTHER READING

A New Magna Carta? House of Commons Political and Constitutional Reform Committee, Second Report of Session 2014–15, 3 July 2014 – you can download the PDF of the report at www.publications.parliament.uk/pa/cm201415/cmselect/cmpolcon/463/463.pdf. Don't be put off by its length – 425 pages! At this stage, just read pages 19–28 which set out the arguments for and against a codified constitution.

www.independent.co.uk/news/uk/politics/uk-should-consider-a-written-constitution-says-top-judge-lord-neuberger-9792250.html – an article in which Lord Neuberger, the President of the UK Supreme Court (the UK's most senior judge), explains in a speech to the 2014 Legal Wales conference why he thinks it is time for the UK to have a codified constitution.

www.supremecourt.uk/docs/speech-141010.pdf – the full text of Lord Neuberger's speech above. The Supreme Court's website is a valuable resource, as it contains not only the full text, and summaries, of important constitutional case law, but also speeches given by Supreme Court judges, which often discuss issues of constitutional significance.

www.glamorgancenturions.co.uk/constitution.html – the constitution of South Wales' finest amateur cricket club.

www.usconstitution.net/const.html – the Constitution of the United States of America, with details of all subsequent amendments.

www.theguardian.com/us-news/gun-control – a constantly updated collection of news stories relating to the ongoing debate about gun control in the USA.

COMPANION WEBSITE

An online glossary compiled by the author is available on the companion website: www.routledge.com/cw/beginningthelaw

Chapter 3
Sources of UK constitutional law

LEARNING OBJECTIVES

After reading this chapter, you should be able to:

* Recognise that the UK's constitution consists of both legal and non-legal rules, and explain the difference between conventions and law
* Identify the different sources of UK constitutional law and understand the difference between primary and secondary legislation
* Define when legislation, or case law, is of constitutional importance
* Understand the importance of conventions in supplementing the law and their inherent flexibility.

INTRODUCTION

We saw in the last chapter that the UK has an uncodified constitution – in other words, it has rules which establish and regulate the Government, but those rules have not been organised into a single document labelled 'the constitution'.

We also saw that laws such as the **Human Rights Act 1998**, which might be regarded as sufficiently important to be 'constitutional' (and are considered as such by the judges – see the discussion of the *Thoburn* (2002) case below and in Chapter 6) have no special status in UK law. They are made, changed and repealed in the same way as any other law.

All of this makes it a little more difficult than it is in other countries to identify with precision and certainty which UK laws are constitutional and which are not. But do not despair! In this chapter we will examine the different sources in which you can find the UK's constitution and will give some guidance as to which rules can fairly be said to have constitutional significance.

LEGAL AND NON-LEGAL RULES

We saw in Chapter 2 that Wheare defined a constitution as 'the collection of rules which establish and regulate… the government'. Not all of these rules take the form of laws. What is the difference between a rule which is a law and one which is not?

Laws

A law is a rule which is enforceable in the courts. This means that if a law is broken, a citizen who suffers as a result can go to the courts and complain about it. If the courts agree that the law has been broken, they can award a remedy to the complainant (whether in the form of money as compensation for their loss or an order making the law-breaker do, or stop doing, something). Where the law which has been broken is a criminal offence, the courts can also penalise the offender, whether by imposing a fine or (in more serious cases) a prison sentence. We examine the remedies available to citizens for breaches of constitutional law in more detail in Chapter 8, where we discuss **judicial review**.

Laws are made by bodies that have authority over the people of the state in which they are enforced. In some countries (e.g. Sudan), this authority was seized by, and is retained by, military force, with laws being imposed on the people 'for the good of the nation'. This is known as a **dictatorship**. In other countries, the authority to make law is bestowed on politicians by the people of the country voting in elections. This is known as a **democracy**. The UK is generally considered around the world to be a democracy, although you can decide for yourself when you have finished reading this book just how democratic its constitution really is!

Laws in the UK take two forms – legislation and case law. Legislation is made by Parliament, whose composition is discussed in Chapter 5. It is important to note at this stage that, of the three elements which make up Parliament (the House of Commons, House of Lords and the Queen), only the House of Commons is currently elected. Case law is made by judges, who are unelected – the method by which they are appointed is discussed in Chapter 8.

Non-legal rules

Not all rules have the force of law. Some rules arise not by imposition from some higher authority (whether elected or not), but from people behaving in a particular way which they recognise is to their common benefit. Once this pattern of behaviour becomes the established norm, so that deviation from it attracts criticism or disapproval, it can be said to be a 'rule'.

Consider, for example, the social rule that we hold open doors for each other. We do this not because it is a law (it is not!), but because life is easier if we all behave like that – we hold doors open for others in the hope that they will do so for us, not because of any legal sanctions that may follow if we do not. If you were walking out of your University library, carrying a heavy load of books in both arms, you would (to say the least!) be disappointed if the person in front of you did not hold open the door for you so that it swung shut in your face. You might drop the books all over the floor, causing yourself considerable embarrassment and irritation. You might think that the person who had failed to hold the door open is incredibly rude. But you could not claim against them in a court for this – the 'rule' that we hold open doors for each other is not legally enforceable.

The rules which make up the UK constitution include a number of very important non-legal rules. They are called **conventions** and they are observed by the key players in the constitution for so long as they are generally considered to be essential to the functioning of the state. Whereas laws are written down, whether in an Act of Parliament or a report of a court's judgment in a particular case, non-legal rules and conventions tend to be unwritten.

We will examine some of the UK's most important constitutional conventions below, and again in Chapters 4 and 7. First, we will identify the different sources of UK constitutional laws.

Primary legislation

Legislation is written-down law made by a legislative body. It is important to distinguish between primary legislation and secondary legislation.

Primary legislation consists of statutes made (or 'enacted') by Parliament (i.e. the House of Commons, the House of Lords and the Queen). They are known as **Acts of Parliament**. We will look in detail at how they are enacted in Chapter 5.

Many Acts of Parliament have direct constitutional significance, e.g.:

- **Parliament Acts 1911 and 1949**.
- **European Communities Act 1972**.
- **Police and Criminal Evidence Act 1984**.
- **Human Rights Act 1998**.
- **Scotland Act 1998**.
- **Anti-Terrorism, Crime and Security Act 2001**.
- **Government of Wales Act 2006**.

The impact of these Acts on the UK's constitution will be examined in detail later on in this book. The process by which primary legislation is enacted, amended and repealed is (with one minor exception, which we will consider in Chapter 5) the same, irrespective of the purpose and subject-matter of that legislation. We have already seen that this distinguishes the UK's constitution from that of, for example, the USA or Germany, where special law-making procedures must be observed in order to change the constitution.

Another key aspect in which the UK's constitution differs from those countries is that, traditionally, the UK's courts have been unable to amend or set aside Acts of Parliament. This is known as the doctrine of **Parliamentary sovereignty** and forms the subject of Chapter 6 of this book.

Not all Acts of Parliament have constitutional importance. Few constitutional lawyers would consider, for example, that the Sunday Trading (London Olympic Games and Paralympic Games) Act 2012 is an act of major constitutional significance. But since all Acts are made the same way, it can be difficult to tell, and with other Acts (e.g. the Firearms (Amendment) Act 1997, discussed in Chapter 2), opinion differs.

Perhaps the most authoritative definition of a '**constitutional statute**' was coined by a judge, LJ Laws, in the case of *Thoburn v Sunderland City Council* (2002):

Key Definition

Constitutional statute: 'a constitutional statute is one which (a) conditions the legal relationship between citizen and State in some general, overarching manner, or (b) enlarges or diminishes the scope of what we would now regard as fundamental constitutional rights'.

LJ Laws, *Thoburn v Sunderland City Council* [2002] EWHC 195

We will return to this important case in Chapter 6.

Secondary legislation

Most of the legislation made in the UK is secondary (also known as 'delegated' or 'subordinate') legislation. Secondary legislation is made (or 'enacted') in the form of **Statutory Instruments**, often with the title 'Regulations' or 'Order'. In 2015, there were 2,059 statutory instruments made in the UK and only 37 Acts of Parliament.

The reason for this is that, as the pace of social and technological change increases, Parliament simply does not have enough time to make all the laws that the UK needs. So, typically, an Act of Parliament establishes a broad framework of principles in relation to a particular matter, and then delegates powers to other bodies to make more detailed laws to fill in the detail required to make those principles work.

Secondary legislation is made by UK Government Ministers. In Scotland and Wales, secondary legislation is also made by the Scottish Executive and the Welsh Ministers using powers given to them by the Scottish Parliament and National Assembly for Wales respectively – you will read more about this in Chapter 6.

Unlike Acts of Parliament, secondary legislation can be challenged in the courts on the basis that it is outside the powers conferred by the enabling Act under whose authority it was made, is in breach of EU law (see below) or is in breach of the **Human Rights Act 1998** (see Chapter 9).

Example

Section 3 of the **Government of Wales Act 2006 (GOWA 2006)** provides that an ordinary general election to the National Assembly for Wales shall be held every four years, from 2007, on the first Thursday in May. This is a provision of primary legislation.

Section 4 GOWA 2006 allows the Secretary of State for Wales to change the election date by up to one month, by making an Order in the form of a statutory instrument. Section 4 itself is a provision of primary legislation, but any date-changing Order made by the Secretary of State would be secondary legislation.

If the Secretary of State made an Order changing the date of the next Assembly election to 1 July 2019, the courts could set aside that Order as invalid. The Order would be illegal as the Secretary of State only has power under s 4 GOWA 2006 to vary the election date by up to one month. In order for the Secretary of State to delay the election by more than one month, Parliament would have to pass another Act giving him power to make such an Order.

Case law

Case law, also known as the common law, is the body of recorded judicial precedent. As individual disputes are brought before the courts, the judges' decisions develop the body of common law on a case-by-case basis. A key function of a constitution is to regulate the relationship between private individuals and the state. Sometimes, cases arise which result in decisions laying down principles of constitutional importance.

Even in countries with codified constitutions, case law is important as it falls to the courts to interpret and apply the constitution in the event of a dispute – see the German case of *Bundesverfassungsgericht* (2006) in the previous chapter. What is unusual about the UK is that key principles which would normally be imposed on the courts by a codified constitution have instead been developed by the courts themselves, and that such cases can be overridden by Acts of Parliament (see Chapter 6).

Judicial review, which we will study in Chapter 8, is an example of a key constitutional principle (or set of principles) which has been developed by the courts. It is a common law doctrine, though it is also related to the principle of Parliamentary sovereignty (see Chapters 6 and 8).

Another example of a case developing the body of constitutional law is set out below:

KEY CASE: *M v Home Office* **[1993] 3 All ER 537**

Background:

M, an asylum seeker, was due to be deported from the UK to Zaire. His lawyer appealed against the decision, and the judge ordered that M should not be deported until the appeal had been heard. Despite this, the Home Office (the Government Department responsible for the matter) deported him. The House of Lords held that an Order (called an 'injunction') issued by the court requiring the Home Secretary (the Government Minister in charge of the Home Office) to return M to the UK was valid, and that having failed to obey the Order, the Home Secretary was in contempt of court.

Principles:

(1) a court may issue an injunction against a Minister of the Crown; and
(2) a Minister failing to comply with such an injunction is in contempt of court.

On-the-spot question

Can you explain the reasoning for the decision in *M v Home Office* by reference to the separation of powers and the rule of law?

Again, many cases (e.g. those involving contract, crime or property law) have no particular constitutional significance, but applying LJ Laws' definition in *Thoburn* (2002), those which fundamentally affect key individual rights or the relationship between citizen and the State do.

From a practical point of view, such cases are often reported with the word 'constitution' or 'constitutional' in the keywords to the case report headnote. So a search on an electronic database such as Westlaw or LexisLibrary for cases including a keyword with the root 'constitution' – together, of course, with any more specific information about the area of law you are researching! – will help to identify important decisions.

European Union law

European Union (EU) law was incorporated into domestic UK law by virtue of Parliament enacting the **European Communities Act 1972 (ECA 1972)**.

EU law confers significant rights on UK citizens, and corresponding obligations on public authorities, as well as private companies and individuals, e.g. the European Commission has issued a number of anti-discrimination Directives in the field of employment law.

The effect of **s 2 ECA 1972** is that rights which are sufficiently clear, precise and unconditional have 'direct effect', i.e. they can be enforced by UK citizens in national courts irrespective of whether they are contained (or contradicted) in UK primary or secondary legislation.

So, in a sense, key individual rights now enter our constitution direct from the EU – but on a legal analysis, they only do so because of s 2 ECA 1972, i.e. they pass into our constitution through a door which has been opened (and which could be shut) by the UK Parliament. This is a contentious area which we will examine further in Chapter 6, where we discuss Parliamentary sovereignty and the forthcoming referendum on the UK's membership of the EU.

European Convention on Human Rights
The European Convention on Human Rights (the Convention) contains substantive rights and freedoms (e.g. right to liberty, freedom of expression) which are recognised in the codified constitutions of most other countries as key constitutional rights. Some of these rights have now been incorporated into UK law by the **Human Rights Act 1998 (HRA 1998)**.

HRA 1998 (like ECA 1972) is included in LJ Laws' list of constitutional statutes and has had a profound impact on the UK's constitution, in particular on the relationships between Parliament, the Government and the courts. As with ECA 1972, HRA 1998 could be repealed, removing these 'fundamental' rights and freedoms from our constitution. It is the policy of the current Government to repeal HRA 1998 and to replace it with a British Bill of Rights, although it is currently unclear what that Bill might contain. We will return to these issues in Chapters 6 and 8.

Some points about terminology – when we talk about human rights such as the right to liberty, we are talking about Articles to the Convention, which is an international treaty signed by many different European States. These rights are, in effect, copied and pasted into UK law by their inclusion in Schedule 1 to HRA 1998.

The Convention is therefore a legally binding document – unlike the non-legal rules known as **conventions** (with a small 'c'!) which we discuss below.

Conventions

Key Definition

Conventions: 'certain rules of constitutional behaviour which are considered to be binding by and upon those who operate the Constitution but which are not enforced by the law courts'.

Geoffrey Marshall and Graeme Moodie, *Some Problems of the Constitution* (1971)

The fact that some important, practical rules key to the operation of the State are not codified into laws is not unique to the UK. Around the world, Governments have found it expedient to adopt working practices which sit alongside the constitutional laws by which they are bound. For example, in the USA, the annual State of the Union address given by the President to Congress is not required by any provision of the USA's Constitution or by any other law, but has become a constitutional convention. Conventions are, if you like, the oil which keeps the constitutional machine working. **Sir Ivor Jennings** describes them as 'the flesh which clothes the dry bones of the law'.[1]

If conventions are not legally binding (see the *Jonathan Cape* case in Chapter 7), why do they matter? Jennings says that 'conventions are obeyed because of the political difficulties which follow if they are not'. Consider how, in the UK, the following constitutional conventions supplement the law:

Law		Convention
Royal Assent is required in order to enact a valid Act of Parliament	⇨	The Queen, on the Prime Minister's advice, assents to a Bill which has been approved by the House of Commons and House of Lords
The Queen can choose Government Ministers	⇨	The Queen appoints as Prime Minister the party political leader who commands the support of a majority of the members of the House of Commons, and appoints other Ministers on the Prime Minister's advice

[1] Sir Ivor Jennings, *The Law and the Constitution*, 1963, London: University of London Press.

On-the-spot question

 What do you think would happen if the Queen did not follow these conventions? What legal consequences might there be? What political consequences might there be?

Because they are uncodified, conventions are inherently flexible. The rules depend on consensus for their origin and survival. They evolve to reflect the political morality of the age.

Individual Ministerial responsibility: a changing convention
The convention of individual Ministerial responsibility arose to ensure that Government Ministers (elected politicians) are accountable to Parliament for the actions of their Departments (staffed by unelected civil servants). There used to be an expectation that a Minister was ultimately responsible for their Department's actions, errors and omissions. When it came to light that the Ministry of Agriculture failed to honour a Government promise to return private land known as Crichel Down to its owners in 1954, the responsible Minister, Sir Thomas Dugdale, resigned:

> I, as Minister, must accept full responsibility to Parliament for any mistakes and inefficiency of officials in my Department, just as, when my officials bring off any successes on my behalf, I take full credit for them.
>
> Sir Thomas Dugdale, resigning as Minister for Agriculture, 1954

In recent years, as the size of Government Departments has grown and it has become increasingly unrealistic to expect Ministers to be familiar with everything that their civil servants do, politicians have become much less inclined to take the blame for mistakes.

Consider, for example, the following statement by the Home Secretary (as the Minister responsible for, among other things, asylum and immigration) in 2006:

> The Immigration and Nationality Directorate is not fit for purpose... it's inadequate in terms of its scope... technology, leadership, management systems and processes... It's not my job to manage this department – it's my job to lead this department.
>
> John Reid, *not* resigning as Home Secretary, 2006

So as Departmental Government has evolved, so has the convention of individual Ministerial responsibility, to the point where Ministers are still considered to be duty-bound to account to Parliament for the mistakes of their Departments, but not necessarily to resign for them.

Some people think that this flexibility to adapt to changing circumstances is one of the great virtues of the UK's uncodified constitution. Others think that the lack of clarity about the rules allows our most powerful politicians to make it up as they go along. It is for you to decide which side of this fence you are on as you read this book!

SUMMARY

- Laws are imposed on the citizen from above, although in a democracy the authority to make laws ultimately derives from the consent of the people, expressed by voting in elections.
- UK constitutional law is found in a variety of sources, including both legislation and case law. Elected politicians contribute to the passage of legislation; case law is made by unelected judges.
- Conventions, which are unwritten and non-legally binding, play an important role in setting expectations about how the key players in the UK constitution use their powers. Conventions are flexible and adapt to suit the political consensus of the age.
- **Professor Peter Hennessy**, in evidence to the House of Lords Select Committee on Public Service in 1997, described the UK constitution as follows: 'We are… a back-of-the-envelope nation, certainly in the organisation of the central state.'

As you read this book and learn more about the UK constitution, you may wish to reflect on this statement and consider whether you agree with it.

FURTHER READING

Barnett, H, *Constitutional & Administrative Law*, 11th edn, 2015, London: Routledge – an authoritative and comprehensive text book on constitutional law, ideal for further reading as you develop your knowledge of the subject. Chapter 2 contains a clear and informative discussion of constitutional conventions.

Barber, N, 'Laws and constitutional conventions' (2009) *Law Quarterly Review* 125, 294–309 – this analyses constitutional laws and conventions in terms of a spectrum of formalisation, considering the growth in importance of the Ministerial Code (see below) as an example of conventions crystallising into law.

Barber, N, 'Can Royal Assent be refused on the advice of the Prime Minister?', UK Constitutional Law Blog (25 September 2013), available at http://ukconstitutionallaw.org, an excellent site hosting up-to-the-minute debate between constitutional lawyers and scholars on current issues – a fascinating article about the circumstances in which the Queen might conceivably be advised by Ministers to deny Royal Assent to a Bill which has passed through Parliament. Notable for recognising the role of constitutional law commentators and scholars in contributing to the understanding, interpretation and application of constitutional conventions.

www.cabinetoffice.gov.uk/resource-library/ministerial-code – the Ministerial Code sets out the standards of conduct expected of Government Ministers in the performance of their duties. For a recent controversy about changes made to the Ministerial Code, see the article by George Letsas, referenced below.

Letsas, G, 'The Rule of all Law: a reply to Finnis, Ekins and Verdirame', UK Constitutional Law Blog (26 November 2015), available at http://ukconstitutionallaw.org – this article analyses changes recently made to the Ministerial Code (see above) from a rule of law perspective.

Marshall, G, *Constitutional Conventions: The Rules and Forms of Political Accountability*, 1987, Oxford: Oxford University Press – a thorough, but readable, exploration of the origins, development and importance of constitutional conventions.

COMPANION WEBSITE

An online glossary compiled by the author is available on the companion website: www.routledge.com/cw/beginningthelaw

Chapter 4

Analysing the UK constitution

LEARNING OBJECTIVES

After reading this chapter, you should be able to:

- Explain the reasoning behind the theory of the separation of powers and compare this theory with the reality of the UK's constitution
- Identify aspects of the UK's constitution which arguably do not conform to the rule of law
- Use 'traffic light' theory as a lens through which to recognise and evaluate different perspectives on the constitution, including your own.

INTRODUCTION

We saw in Chapter 3 that the UK's uncodified constitution is found in a variety of sources. Some of the most important rules of the constitution are unwritten and unenforceable. Even the legal rules can be difficult to identify with certainty as 'constitutional' – consider the question we posed in Chapter 2 about whether the Firearms (Amendment) Act 1997 changed the UK's constitution. Does the definition of a 'constitutional statute' which we examined in Chapter 3 provide a clear answer to this question?

Ultimately, the answers to questions like these depend on your perspective. This book encourages you to develop your own views on the UK's constitution and your examiner will like it if you can articulate them clearly in your essays. To help you to develop your own informed and credible perspective, we will now explore some ideas, theories and doctrines which you can use as lenses through which to examine the specific laws and conventions discussed in the rest of this book.

SEPARATION OF POWERS – THEORY

We looked briefly at the doctrine of the separation of powers in Chapter 2. The essence of the doctrine, as defined by Montesquieu, is that the State comprises three branches – the legislature who make the law, the executive who govern the country and the courts who settle disputes. Montesquieu thought that in order to prevent tyranny (i.e. the concentration of excessive power in a single person or body), these three institutions must be separate from each other, in terms both of having exclusive competence to perform their respective functions and of having their own personnel.

The archetypal expression of Montesquieu's doctrine is found in the USA's Constitution. The President heads the executive, acting within the legal and financial limits set by Congress, the validity of which can be tested in the Supreme Court. While Montesquieu based his theory on his own personal interpretation of the UK's constitutional arrangements, in reality there is much less of a clear separation of powers within the UK.

SEPARATION OF POWERS – REALITY

Examiners often ask you to discuss the extent to which the UK constitution conforms to Montesquieu's doctrine of the separation of powers. This requires you to examine the relationship between each branch of the State (i.e. legislature/executive, legislature/judiciary and executive/judiciary) in detail.

At this stage in this book, we are not yet in a position to do that. Later chapters will explore the make-up, functions and powers of Parliament (the legislature), the Government (the executive) and the courts, as well as the constitutional dynamics between these institutions. But it is important to realise, right at the outset, that you need to take a critical approach to your study of the constitution (and, indeed, law in general). Lawyers do not simply accept what they are told at face value. They test the evidence.

Consider the following extract from a judgment given in 1980 by Lord Diplock, at the time one of the UK's most senior judges and a member of its highest court (then, the House of Lords):

> It cannot be too strongly emphasised that the British constitution, though largely unwritten, is firmly based on the separation of powers. Parliament makes the laws, the judiciary interpret them.
>
> Lord Diplock, *Duport Steels v Sirs* [1980] 1 WLR 142

A critical examination of this statement requires an assessment of the constitutional relationship between Parliament, the Government and the courts at the time. This reveals that, despite Lord Diplock's assertion that the constitution is 'firmly based on the separation of powers', there were in fact considerable overlaps between:

- Parliament and the Government – the key members of whom, i.e. the Prime Minister and her Cabinet colleagues, were also members of the House of Commons (more about these institutions in Chapters 5 and 8).
- Parliament and the courts – the most senior court in the UK, the House of Lords, was physically located within Parliament and comprised Law Lords with a dual role as both judges and as legislators. While conventions discouraged the Law Lords from participating and voting in debates on contentious matters before Parliament, no law precluded them from doing so.

So the UK's constitution was not as 'firmly based' on a separation of powers as it first appears from reading Lord Diplock's statement.

Enactment of the **Human Rights Act 1998** was a game-changing moment for the UK constitution. In effect, it made it illegal (through its incorporation into UK law of **Article 6 of the European Convention on Human Rights** and case law under that provision) for the fusion of the legislature and judiciary to continue. We will discuss this further in Chapters 6 and 8.

The effect is that the UK's constitution now clearly separates the judiciary from both the executive and the legislature, both in form as well as in substance. There remain, however, significant overlaps between Parliament and Government, both in terms of personnel (with the Prime Minister and most of the Cabinet being drawn from the House of Commons) and function (as we have seen, most UK legislation is now made by Government Ministers using powers delegated to them by Parliament). See **diagram entitled 'The UK constitution at a glance' on page 11** to which you should keep returning as you graft more detail onto your knowledge of the constitution.

Opinions differ as to the extent to which this 'matters' in terms of evaluating the UK's constitution. Walter Bagehot, a Victorian constitutional scholar, considered the overlap between Parliament and Government to be the 'efficient secret'[1] of the UK's constitution, because it allows the party (or coalition of parties, as in the 2010 General Election) which wins a majority of seats in a General Election to the House of Commons to pass laws which enable it to fulfil its promise to electors. Bagehot sees this as profoundly democratic.

On the other hand, Lord Hailsham (Lord Chancellor and Cabinet Minister during the 1970s and 1980s) described the relationship between Government and Parliament as an 'elective dictatorship',[2] in which the party that wins control of the House of Commons has, in effect, absolute law-making power until the next General Election.

---

[1] Walter Bagehot, *The English Constitution*, P Smith (ed), 2010, Cambridge: Cambridge University Press.
[2] Lord Hailsham, *Elective Dictatorship, The Richard Dimbleby Lecture*, 1976, London: BBC.

As you read this book and learn more about Parliament, the Government and the courts, think about which of these views you prefer. This will help you to develop a coherent approach to writing essays on topics such as Parliamentary sovereignty, the impact and possible repeal of the Human Rights Act 1998, codification of the constitution, conventions and the constitutional role of judicial review – all of which will be discussed in detail in the remaining chapters.

THE RULE OF LAW

We saw in Chapter 2 that the concept of the rule of law encompasses both a legal definition (as set out by Dicey, involving equality, consistency and due process) and a wider definition (articulated by Dworkin) in which law ultimately depends for its validity on the obedience of the people to whom the law applies; this in turn depends on the laws which seek to regulate those people being just, fair and commanding their respect.

Tom Bingham, the former Lord Chief Justice, says that the rule of law is 'the nearest we are likely to approach to a universal secular religion', while acknowledging that for some politicians it amounts to little more than 'Hooray for our side'[3] – meaning that the legislative and judicial process can be exploited by powerful groups to legitimise measures which prioritise their particular interests.

As you read the chapters of this book, think about the extent to which key doctrines, statutes and cases conform to either of these concepts of the rule of law. For example:

Topic	Chapter	Rule of law issue
Parliamentary sovereignty	6	Should Parliament be able to pass any law that it wishes or should it be subject to some 'higher laws'?
Impact of HRA 1998	6	Do **ss 3 and 4 HRA 1998** give too much, or too little, power to unelected judges to review Acts of Parliament?
Prerogative powers	7	Is it acceptable that some key Government powers are ill-defined, do not derive from a democratic legislature and are not subject to full judicial control?
Conventions	7	Should all the important rules of the constitution be codified, so that they are clear, accessible and enforceable?
Judicial review	8	Have the judges gone too far (or not far enough) in developing extra-statutory tests for the validity of executive action, such as irrationality and the principles of natural justice?

---

3 Tom Bingham, *The Rule of Law*, 2010, London: Penguin.

You should also think about the relationship between the rule of law and the separation of powers. In Montesquieu's pure model of the doctrine, the separation of powers complements the rule of law as the executive depends upon the legislature for authority to act, with the courts policing the legal boundaries. As we have already seen, however, the UK's uncodified constitution involves more complex relationships. While the rule of law and the separation of powers are far from mutually exclusive, the extent to which one or other doctrine is prioritised by a particular judge differs:

KEY CASE: *R v A* [2001] 3 All ER 1

Background:

Section 41(3)(c) of the Youth Justice and Criminal Evidence Act 1999 limited the circumstances in which a defendant could cross-examine a rape complainant about a previous sexual relationship. The House of Lords had to decide whether **s 3 of the Human Rights Act 1998** required them to interpret that provision in a way which gave effect to the right to a fair trial contained in **Article 6 of the European Convention on Human Rights (the Convention)**.

Principle:

The House of Lords, in effect, relied on **s 3 HRA 1998** to 'read in' the words 'subject to a fair trial', so as to construe s 41 compatibly with Article 6 of the Convention. This meant interpreting the provision so as to allow the cross-examination of rape complainants.

Lord Steyn:

> In accordance with the will of Parliament it will sometimes be necessary to adopt an interpretation which linguistically will appear strained. The techniques to be used will not only involve the reading down of express language in a statute but also the reading down of provisions. A declaration of incompatibility is a measure of last resort and must be avoided unless it is plainly impossible to do so.

Lord Hope:

> [Section 3 HRA 1998 is] only a rule of interpretation. It does not entitle the judges to act as legislators... the compatibility is to be achieved only so far as this is possible. Plainly this will not be possible if the legislation contains provisions which expressly contradict the meaning which the enactment would have to be given to make it compatible.

It is possible to view this judicial discussion as a contest between two great heavyweights of constitutional thinking, with Lord Steyn fighting for the rule of law (i.e. the idea that the right to a fair trial is a principle of 'higher law', with which Parliament must be assumed to have intended to comply) and Lord Hope in the opposite corner defending the separation of powers (by denying the right of unelected judges to interfere in Parliamentary legislation).

In the end, Lord Steyn's view prevailed among three of the five judges. We will return to this important case in Chapter 6. For now, the point to take on board is that there is room for differences of opinion, even at the highest level of judicial intellectual reasoning. You should see this as very liberating! If the finest legal minds in the country cannot agree about a particular question of constitutional law, why should you and your fellow students (or you and your lecturer)?

In exams, provided that you can write balanced essays which recognise and explain competing points of view, you are quite entitled (and encouraged!) to say which view you prefer and why. Further guidance on how to answer exam questions is given in Chapter 11.

'TRAFFIC LIGHT' THEORY

This is a theory, developed by the constitutional scholars **Carol Harlow and Richard Rawlings**,[4] which emphasises the importance of political perspective in evaluating a system of constitutional law. The different colours of the traffic light represent different approaches to the relationship between the executive (i.e. the Government, or other public authorities) and the courts.

'Red light' theory

Advocates of the red light theory regard the Government as a potential threat to civil liberties and favour minimum Government intervention in people's lives. They see constitutional law as a means of controlling the State, and protecting the rights and freedoms of individuals.

'Green light' theory

Advocates of the green light theory see the Government institutions and public authorities as the embodiment of community values and co-operation. They see constitutional law less as a means of limiting and controlling Government than as a

4 C Harlow and R Rawlings, *Law and Administration*, 2009, Cambridge: Cambridge University Press.

means of empowering Government to implement welfare and social reforms for the good of the public.

'Amber light' theory

Amber light perspectives consider that the purpose of constitutional law is to secure a basic framework of individual rights and freedoms, but, subject to those limits, to allow Government a substantial amount of power. This 'middle ground' approach is perhaps best reflected in Parliament's unique approach to incorporation of the **Convention** via **the Human Rights Act 1998**. We will discuss this further in Chapters 6 and 8.

The following recent Supreme Court decision draws together everything that you have read about in this chapter. It is another example of how the highest judges in the land can take fundamentally different approaches to the relative priority to be given to competing principles of constitutional law.

KEY CASE: *R (Evans) v Attorney General* **[2015] UKSC 21**

Background:

Mr Evans, a journalist for *The Guardian* newspaper, challenged the decision of the Attorney General (the chief legal advisor to the UK Government – see **Chapter 7**) to issue a certificate under s 53(2) of the **Freedom of Information Act 2000** to the effect that various Government Departments were entitled not to disclose to Mr Evans correspondence between them and the Prince of Wales (the 'black spider' memos), despite a judicial decision by the Upper Tribunal that the correspondence should be disclosed. The Attorney General argued that he was entitled to issue such a certificate, notwithstanding the Upper Tribunal's decision, because Parliament had given him the power to do so on 'reasonable grounds', and he considered that there were 'reasonable grounds' to veto disclosure in the public interest, principally because he considered that the future King should be able to enter into a private dialogue with the Government.

Principle:

The Supreme Court held by a 5:2 majority that the Attorney General's issue of the s 53(2) certificate to veto disclosure of the correspondence was unlawful. What is particularly interesting to constitutional lawyers is the fundamental differences in approach taken by the Supreme Court judges.

Lords Neuberger, Reed and Kerr based their decision to quash the Attorney General's certificate on fundamental, high-level constitutional principles. In particular, they considered that it would contravene the rule of law for the executive to use the s 53 power to override a judicial decision. Lord Neuberger considered that it is 'fundamental to the rule of law that decisions and actions of the executive are… reviewable by the court at the suit of an interested citizen' and that 'section 53, as interpreted by the Attorney General's argument in this case… stands [that] principle on its head'.

By contrast, Lords Wilson and Hughes (who gave the minority opinions) considered that the Attorney General had acted within the power granted to him by the legislature, via the 'plain words' of s 53. Their opinions prioritise the separation of powers and the doctrine of Parliamentary sovereignty (see **Chapter 6**). Lord Hughes said that 'it is an integral part of the rule of law that courts give effect to Parliamentary intention'. Lord Wilson pointed out that the s 53 power is exercised by a politician, accountable to Parliament and to the electorate for his use of that power. Where Parliament had seen fit to grant the veto power to the executive, the sanctions for its use should be political rather than judicial.

Lord Mance and Lady Hale took the middle ground. Their approach was to scrutinise the reasonableness of the Attorney General's use of the s 53 power based on traditional, administrative law principles (see the sections on judicial review in **Chapter 8**). They considered that it was, in principle, open to the legislature to grant the executive a power to veto judicial decisions on closely defined grounds, but that it was for the court to apply a particularly intense level of scrutiny in reviewing whether those grounds were satisfied in any particular case. This approach respects both the separation of powers and the rule of law, and seeks to balance the competing doctrines.

On-the-spot question

 Applying the traffic light theory you have read about above, how would you characterise the differing approaches of the Supreme Court judges in *R (Evans) v Attorney General* (2015)?

SUMMARY

- Knowing the key cases and legislation is only half the battle in constitutional law. If you can explain the reasons behind the law by reference to the 'bigger picture' of the constitution, you will write better essays and get higher marks.

- The separation of powers and the rule of law are key constitutional doctrines. You need to know the definitions of these doctrines, and be able to evaluate the extent to which key judicial decisions and statutory provisions conform to them.
- The separation of powers requires the legislature, the executive and the judiciary to be separate both in function and personnel. The purpose of the doctrine is to prevent one branch of the State from exercising too much power. The UK does not exhibit a complete separation of powers, particularly between Parliament and Government, where there is considerable overlap. We will discuss the consequences of this in the following chapters.
- The rule of law is based on notions of equality, consistency and procedural fairness. It requires Government to derive its authority from clear and accessible legal sources. As we will see, the extent to which some areas of the UK's constitution conform to the rule of law is questionable.
- The doctrines of the separation of powers and the rule of law can sometimes conflict. Even in the Supreme Court, different judges prioritise the doctrines differently in particular cases.
- 'Traffic light' theory can help you both to develop your own perspective on the UK's constitution, and to recognise and evaluate the perspectives of other students, academics, politicians and judges.

FURTHER READING

Benwell, R and Gay, O, *The Separation of Powers* (15 August 2011), available at http://research-briefings.files.parliament.uk/documents/SN06053/SN06053.pdf – this is a paper prepared by researchers working in the House of Commons Library to brief MPs. It is a concise explanation of the doctrine of the separation of powers, and the extent to which it is reflected in the UK's constitution.

Bingham, T, *The Rule of Law*, 2011, London: Penguin – winner of the Orwell Prize for Best Political Book 2011, this is a concise, highly readable account by the UK's former Lord Chief Justice – like a 'greatest hits' of the rule of law! An excellent place to start your further reading on this difficult topic.

Harlow, C and Rawlings, R, *Law and Administration*, 2009, Cambridge: Cambridge University Press – more advanced, and recommended as a 'next step' once you have finished this book and are familiar with the institutions and key rules of the UK's constitution. It examines the relationship between the courts, Government and Parliament in a social and political context.

www.telegraph.co.uk/comment/columnists/philipjohnston/8001383/Do-we-want-to-be-ruled-by-judges-or-MPs.html – a thought-provoking article on the separation of powers and the role of the judiciary.

www.judiciary.gov.uk/wp-content/uploads/2015/06/speech-by-lj-beatson-new-model-judiciary1. pdf – a speech by Lord Justice Beatson (a Court of Appeal judge), based on talks given at the

Hart Judicial Review Conference in December 2014 and at the University of York Law School in May 2015. It examines the relationship between the judiciary and the executive from a practical perspective.

www.judiciary.gov.uk/wp-content/uploads/2015/09/speech-lcj-judicial-independence-in-a-changing-constitutional-landscape.pdf – another judicial speech, this time by Lord Chief Justice Thomas in September 2015, the theme of which is that 'judicial independence must not mean judicial isolation'. It is perhaps worth comparing and contrasting with Lord Justice Beatson's speech above. To what extent is Lord Chief Justice Thomas prioritising the rule of law over the separation of powers?

http://publiclawforeveryone.com/2015/07/07/the-uk-supreme-court-and-the-british-constitution – Mark Elliott is Professor of Public Law at the University of Cambridge. His blog is regularly updated and provides highly readable material on key constitutional cases. In this post, he analyses the Supreme Court's decision in **R (Evans) v Attorney General** (2015).

COMPANION WEBSITE

An online glossary compiled by the author is available on the companion website: www.routledge.com/cw/beginningthelaw

Chapter 5
Parliament's functions and make-up

LEARNING OBJECTIVES

After reading this chapter, you should be able to:

- Accurately describe the functions and composition of Parliament
- Explain how Parliament makes law
- Understand how MPs are elected to the House of Commons
- Discuss the pros and cons of different voting systems for General Elections
- Form your own view on whether changes to the House of Lords are necessary.

INTRODUCTION

Parliament is the most powerful element in the UK's uncodified constitution.

As you will see in Chapter 6, Parliament is the supreme law-maker. Acts of Parliament have changed the constitution, reversed decisions of our highest court, made laws for countries thousands of miles away, and incorporated both European Union law on free trade and the European Convention on Human Rights into our national body of law, so that we can rely on them in local courts.

For centuries, the courts accepted and applied Acts of Parliament without question and without exception. This judicial obedience to the will of Parliament is known as **Parliamentary sovereignty**. As you will discover in Chapter 6, while Parliamentary sovereignty remains the defining feature of the UK's uncodified constitution, some recent legal and political developments have challenged the traditional notion of a Parliament which is *absolutely* sovereign.

There have also been suggestions in recent years that Parliament has been subordinated by Government. We will explore the relationship between Parliament and Government in Chapter 7. In theory, Parliament exists to empower, but also to restrict, the Government Ministers who run the country. Parliament is supposed to hold the Government to account for its policies, its spending and its actions, and to 'keep individual Ministers honest'. We will analyse the degree to which Parliament is able to perform this key constitutional function and will ask whether the current electoral and political system adequately equips Parliament to do what is expected of it.

Both Parliamentary sovereignty and the relationship between Parliament and Government are favourite topics of examiners. Usually, you can expect an essay question on at least one (if not both!) of these topics on your examination paper. Chapters 5–7 of this book will help you to write about either topic with confidence, demonstrating knowledge of the key case law and legislation, and an understanding of the political context in which they are decided and enacted.

Before we can explore these topics in detail, it is vital that you understand what Parliament is and how it works – because in order to write an informed essay about the power of Parliament, whether in relation to the courts or to the Government, you need to understand that the political and legal respect afforded to Parliament depends on its democratic credentials. To do well in this area, you also need to be able to look at Parliament's structure and procedures critically, and ask whether Parliament is democratic enough, or whether reform is needed in order to make it better able to perform the constitutional role with which it is entrusted.

We will begin by looking briefly at the origins and evolution of Parliament, before moving on to a detailed consideration of its current functions and composition.

THE EVOLUTION OF PARLIAMENT

Early Parliaments

The word 'Parliament' derives from the French word *parler* ('to speak'). The earliest Parliaments took place in the thirteenth century and were ad hoc events in which the King summoned his closest religious and military advisers so that he could consult them about issues of Government such as finance. This body of aristocratic noblemen (lords temporal) and bishops (lords spiritual) is the forerunner to today's **House of Lords**.

The King's advisers were often wealthy and powerful in their own right, and as their influence grew, they demanded more regular meetings with the King and more concessions in return for their financial and political support. In 1215, King John signed **Magna Carta**, a charter of legal rights forced on him by the barons in which he subjected the monarchy to the law of the land – an important development, as before that it was thought that the monarch was appointed by God and was therefore all-powerful.

After a dispute between King Henry III and Simon de Montfort about the frequency with which Parliament met, the new King Edward I established regular meetings of Parliament which included not only nobles and churchmen, but also representatives of each county, town and city known as 'commoners'. During the reign of Edward III (1327–77), these local representatives began to sit in a separate chamber known as the **House of Commons** and to demand greater influence over the King's Government of the country.

Parliament's influence grows

By the mid-fifteenth century, the King depended on the co-operation of the House of Commons, both to raise taxes and to make new laws. Henry VIII's Reformation Parliament sat from 1529 to 1536 and passed a series of laws which radically changed the nature, doctrine and authority of the Church, revolutionised the economy by transferring vast amounts of Church land and property to the Government, and altered the line of succession to the throne. Royal authority now found its expression through law made in and with the consent of Parliament.

This co-operation between monarchy and Parliament broke down during the reign of Charles I (1625–49) who, after a series of financial and religious disputes, tried to 'go it alone', relying on ancient powers under the **Royal Prerogative** (see Chapter 7) to rule without Parliament for 11 years. This culminated in a Civil War (1642–51), following which Charles I was executed, and Oliver Cromwell, leader of Parliament, briefly established a republican Commonwealth, in which the remaining members of the House of Commons formed a 'Rump Parliament', governing without the monarchy or the House of Lords.

After Cromwell died, the monarchy was restored to power, but further religious disputes led to the 1688 Glorious Revolution and the defeat of James II. Parliament now asserted its power over the monarchy through the **Bill of Rights 1689**, which established a constitutional framework within which the monarchy was to operate, preventing the monarch from creating or suspending laws, raising taxes or keeping an army without Parliament's consent; and the **Act of Settlement 1701**, in which Parliament clarified the line of succession to the throne and safeguarded the independence of judges by protecting their salaries and granting them security of tenure, ensuring that they could not be removed from office for political reasons.

The **Acts of Union 1707**, in effect, abolished the independent sovereign Parliaments of England and Scotland, creating a new Parliament of Great Britain. Aspects of the Act of Union remain controversial – see Chapter 6, where we will also discuss the effect of the recent devolution of law-making powers to the **Scottish Parliament** and the **National Assembly for Wales**.

Extending voting rights

During the eighteenth and nineteenth centuries, the social, demographic and economic changes caused by the Industrial Revolution created pressure to broaden the category of people (the 'franchise') allowed to elect members of the House of Commons. Prior to the **Reform Acts 1832 and 1867**, the right to vote was limited and based on land ownership rights. This created a perverse situation where small villages were electing two members of the House of Commons, while growing cities such as Birmingham and Manchester had no representatives. The **Reform Act 1867** doubled the franchise, extending the right to vote to skilled and unskilled male labourers.

Women did not get the right to vote until the **Representation of the People Act 1918** and were not granted the same voting rights as men until the **Equal Franchise Act 1928**. A full and equal franchise, granting a single vote to each man and woman over 21, was not achieved until the **Representation of the People Act 1948.**

Voting rights today

The key statute governing voting rights today is the **Representation of the People Act 1983**, which entitles British citizens over 18 years of age to vote in Parliamentary elections in a single constituency on whose electoral register they appear. There are some exceptions to this general rule[1] – e.g. convicted prisoners in detention are currently not entitled to vote, but this has been challenged recently both in the courts and in Parliament:

KEY CASE: *Hirst v UK* (74025/01), European Court of Human Rights (Grand Chamber), 6 October 2005

Background:

Hirst was a convicted prisoner serving a life sentence for manslaughter. He complained that s 3 of the Representation of the People Act 1983 disqualified him from voting in Parliamentary elections while he was detained, arguing that voting was a right, not a privilege, and that there was no legitimate reason for removing it from prisoners. The UK Government argued that it was reasonable to deprive prisoners of the vote as they had not demonstrated that they were responsible citizens.

Principle:

The Grand Chamber of the European Court of Human Rights held that the UK's blanket ban depriving all prisoners of their right to vote is disproportionate and illegal. Article 3 of the First Protocol to the European Convention on Human Rights gives citizens

---

[1] See e.g. ss 1 and 3 of the Representation of the People Act 1983; s 3 of the House of Lords Act 1999.

the right to vote in free elections. While that right is capable of being lawfully restricted, the restriction contained in s 3 of the Representation of the People Act 1983 takes no account of the seriousness of the offence or the length of the sentence, and demonstrates no rationale for the ban beyond imposing a further punishment on prisoners.

The UK Government challenged this ruling, but was unsuccessful. It was given until 11 October 2011 to bring UK law into line with the European Convention on Human Rights, but has not yet done so. In **Frith and others v UK (2014) All ER (D) 57** and **McHugh and others v UK (2015) ECHR 155** relating to a large number of outstanding claims by prisoners, the European Court of Human Rights noted the UK's continuing violation of Article 3 to Protocol No 1 of the Convention, but did not award the applicants any compensation or legal expenses.

The issue of prisoner voting has become a key battleground in the debate about the UK's incorporation of the European Convention on Human Rights, and the possible repeal of the Human Rights Act 1998, which is considered further in Chapter 6.

For more detail about the key legal principles underlying the European Court of Human Rights' judgment in **Hirst (2005)**, see Chapter 9.

On-the-spot question

Do you think that prisoners should have the right to vote? Are there any circumstances in which you think that it should it be curtailed? Is the UK Government's approach to this issue compatible with the rule of law? The **Further reading** to which you are directed at the end of this chapter will help you to answer this question.

PARLIAMENT'S COMPOSITION TODAY – OVERVIEW

Parliament is composed of three elements:

* the House of Commons;
* the House of Lords; and
* the Queen.

The UK has a 'bicameral' Parliament, i.e. it is made up of two Houses (just as the US legislature, Congress, is made up of the House of Representatives and the Senate). Bicameral institutions arose because of the need to represent different sectors of the population. As we have seen, in the UK, the House of Lords represented the Church and the aristocracy, while the House of Commons traditionally consisted of local representatives known as 'commoners'.

The House of Commons is elected, i.e. its members are chosen by the citizens for whom it makes law. The House of Lords is not – its members are appointed by the Queen, on the advice of the Government. The Queen's role in Parliament is now largely ceremonial – although the monarch still retains important legal powers, such as the right to dismiss Parliament and call a General Election, and the final say in deciding whether a proposal for a new law is enacted as an Act of Parliament (this is known as granting **Royal Assent**). These powers are by convention exercised on the advice of, and at the request of, the **Prime Minister**, an elected politician who is an MP and the Leader of the Government. Their importance is analysed at the end of this chapter.

We will first consider the functions of Parliament, defined on its own website (www.parliament.uk/about/how/role) as:

- examining and challenging the work of the Government (scrutiny);
- debating and passing laws (legislation);
- enabling the Government to raise taxes.

We will then examine the membership of the two Houses in detail and will explore the extent to which the current arrangements for electing members to the House of Commons, and appointing members to the House of Lords, equip Parliament to perform those functions democratically and effectively.

We will also consider the latest failed attempt to reform the House of Lords and a recent debate about changing the voting system for electing members of the House of Commons, in which a proposal to adopt a system called the Alternative Vote was rejected by UK citizens in a public vote known as a **referendum**.

PARLIAMENT'S FUNCTIONS – LEGISLATING

In its combined form of Commons, Lords and Queen ('the Queen in Parliament'), Parliament is the supreme law-maker, enacting (making), amending (changing) and repealing (abolishing) primary legislation in the form of Acts of Parliament.

Overview

Primary legislation starts off as a policy proposal, is then drafted into a form capable of becoming law (a 'Bill') and becomes an Act of Parliament once it has passed through the appropriate Parliamentary process (see below) and has been given Royal Assent by the Queen.

Public Bills

These are proposals for primary legislation that will apply to the general public – e.g. the **Government of Wales Act 2006** or the Dentists Act 1984.

Government Bills are those proposals for legislation adopted by **Cabinet** into the Government's legislative programme. Bills to enact policies which the Government promised to deliver in its election **manifesto** take priority.

Private Members' Bills are non-Government-sponsored Bills introduced by non-ministerial MPs. They often fail for lack of Parliamentary time – an example is the Hunting Bill introduced by a backbench Labour MP which ran out of time in 1998, but was subsequently enacted when re-introduced as a Government Bill in 2004.

Private Bills

These affect only particular people or a particular locality (e.g. the Cardiff Bay Barrage Bill).

Procedure for Public Bills

Bills can be introduced in either House (except for financial measures, which must be introduced in the Commons). The procedural diagram (overleaf) assumes that the Bill has been introduced in the Commons. The policy and principles behind a Bill will often have been published in advance in a **Green Paper** (a consultation document) and then in a **White Paper**, which contains the Government's opinion on how the law should change. Increasingly, Bills are published in draft form to allow some initial scrutiny before being formally introduced to Parliament.

English votes for English laws

In October 2015, MPs voted to change the House of Commons' Standing Orders (its own internal rules) to change the procedure for how Bills which affect only England (or England and Wales) are enacted.

This new procedure is known as English votes for English laws (EVEL). If the Speaker of the House certifies a Bill, or provisions in a Bill, as affecting only England (or England and

Procedure for a Public Bill introduced in the House of Commons

House of Commons

1st reading
Purely formal

2nd reading
Whole House debates general principles

Committee stage
Detailed line-by-line scrutiny by Committee of MPs Committee can amend/remove/add clauses

Report stage
Whole House votes on whether or not to accept amendments proposed in Committee

3rd reading
Final consideration of the amended Bill on a 'take it or leave it' basis

House of Lords

1st reading
Purely formal

2nd reading
Whole House debates general principles

Committee stage
Detailed line-by-line scrutiny. Any Member can take part and propose amendments

Report stage
House votes on whether or not to accept amendments proposed in Committee

3rd reading
Final consideration of the amended Bill on a 'take it or leave it' basis

Ping-Pong?

If the Lords have made any amendments to the Bill in the form passed by the Commons, it can go backwards and forwards until the two Houses reach agreement. See below for procedural devices used to break a deadlock between the Houses

Royal Assent
*By convention, the Queen grants Royal Assent to a Bill approved by both Houses, or a Bill passed using the provisions in the **Parliament Acts 1911 and 1949***

Wales), then the Bill is subject to an additional stage, between Report and Third Reading, which requires a Grand Committee of English (or English and Welsh, as appropriate) MPs to approve the relevant parts of the Bill by voting for a consent motion before the Bill proceeds. Any subsequent amendments to the Bill in the House of Lords are subject to a double majority vote, requiring the consent of (1) English (or English and Welsh) MPs and (2) all MPs before the Bill is submitted for Royal Assent.

EVEL is intended to address a constitutional anomaly. As you will see in Chapter 6, the UK Parliament has devolved law-making powers in certain areas, such as education, health and housing, to Scotland, Wales and Northern Ireland, yet there is no equivalent legislature for England – the UK Parliament legislates for England on those matters. This begs the following question (known as the West Lothian question, because it was first asked by the MP for West Lothian in Scotland, Tam Dalyell):

> Why should MPs from Northern Ireland, Scotland and Wales, sitting in the House of Commons of the United Kingdom, be able to vote on matters that affect only England; while MPs from England are unable to vote on matters that have been devolved to the Northern Ireland Assembly, the Scottish Parliament and the Welsh Assembly?

The UK Government introduced EVEL largely to placate Conservative MPs, and English voters, after the UK Government agreed to grant additional powers to Scotland following the 2014 referendum on Scottish independence in which 55 per cent of those voting decided that Scotland should remain in the UK. EVEL is supposed to provide an answer to the West Lothian question, but it is arguably an incomplete answer and is controversial.

First, EVEL stops short of creating a legislature for England equivalent to the Scottish Parliament or the National Assembly for Wales; instead, it gives English MPs (who stood for election to a UK institution) extra powers on England-only matters. Scottish, Northern Irish and Welsh MPs have argued that this reduces their status to second-class MPs.

Second, the parties currently in opposition have argued that EVEL is a political move designed to engineer a stronger majority for the current Government in relation to English-only matters. Traditionally, the Conservative Party has attracted significantly more support in English constituencies than it has in Scotland or Wales. Reserving the final say on English-only laws for English-only MPs gives the current Government greater control of those matters and makes it harder for a future Government whose majority comprises MPs spread across the UK to enact its policies in England.

The counter-argument is that if a majority of English constituencies vote for one party, it would be undemocratic for them not to be subject to the policies of the party for which they voted, and that people have the opportunity to change how they vote to take account of the new system.

On-the-spot question

? Do you think that EVEL is a pragmatic answer to the West Lothian question? Or do you think it is a temporary political expedient which is unsustainable? Do you think that the introduction of EVEL makes the UK more likely, or less likely, to stay together? The **Further reading** at the end of this chapter will help you to answer this question.

SCRUTINY OF PRIMARY LEGISLATION

> It is all deeply unsatisfactory, and felt to be so by almost everyone involved in it.
>
> Tony Wright MP, *British Politics: A Very Short Introduction*, 2003

House of Commons

Detailed scrutiny of a Bill's provisions takes place in a 'standing committee' specially set up for the Bill, although 'constitutional' Bills such as the **Government of Wales Bill** are scrutinised in a 'Committee of the Whole House'.

Amendments are proposed by way of a formal motion, which is debated and then voted upon. Members usually vote along party lines, and as standing committees reflect the overall proportion of seats each party has in the House, Government defeats are rare.

The Government can also control the amount of time allocated to scrutiny of a Bill by **programme motions** and **guillotines.**

Parliamentary Committees do, however, play an important role both in scrutinising legislation in detail – in particular, to ensure that the proposals actually work – and in holding Ministers to account. Select Committees focus their work on particular policy areas (e.g. defence, banking or constitutional affairs) and operate on a cross-party, more consensual basis. They are well-resourced, and have the powers to compel written and oral evidence from witnesses (e.g. experts on a particular matter). This enables them to access and deploy the expertise necessary to ask searching questions of Ministers about spending, policies and administration.

Reports of Select Committees can exert considerable influence: for example, an adverse report by the Home Affairs Select Committee in 2013[2] precipitated the abolition of the UK Border Agency and the re-organisation of the administration of immigration and visas.

House of Lords

Scrutiny in the House of Lords is less partisan and debate is less adversarial. Government defeats in the House of Lords are more common – the amendments passed in the Lords are then re-submitted to the Commons for further consideration ('ping-pong').

---

[2] *The Work of the UK Border Agency (July–September 2012) – Conclusions and Recommendations*, Home Affairs Select Committee Report, 19 March 2013, available at www.publications.parliament.uk/pa/cm201213/cmselect/cmhaff/792/79207.htm.

RELATIONSHIP BETWEEN THE COMMONS AND THE LORDS

While the House of Lords plays an important role in reviewing and scrutinising legislation (highlighting defects, etc.), important political and legal rules have developed to ensure that the will of the elected Commons prevails in the event of a conflict between the Houses.

Salisbury Convention

This is a non-legally binding political rule that the Lords will accept a legislative proposal which formed part of the Government's election manifesto. In October 2006, a Joint Committee on Conventions, while accepting the primacy of the Commons, rejected a Government proposal to codify this convention. The Liberal Democrats have made it clear that they no longer consider themselves bound by it (e.g. in voting to reject Government proposals for compulsory ID cards during the passage of the **Identity Cards Act 2006**).

Parliament Acts 1911 and 1949

The Parliament Act 1911, as amended by the Parliament Act 1949, places legal limits on the power of the Lords to frustrate the will of the Commons.

The Lords can reject a Bill passed by the Commons in two consecutive Parliamentary sessions, after which the Commons can send it to the Queen for Royal Assent without the Lords' consent.

This ensures that in the event of a conflict, the will of the Commons prevails and the Lords can merely delay, not veto, the passage of the Bill.

Use of the Parliament Acts is rare, but becoming more frequent – they have been relied upon more times (four) in the last 20 years than in the previous 80 years. The most recent example is the **Hunting Act 2004**, after which the House of Lords (in its judicial capacity, the highest appellate court at the time) rejected a challenge to the validity of the Parliament Acts.

KEY CASE: *R (Jackson) v Attorney General* [2005] UKHL 56

Background:

The Hunting Act 2004 banned the hunting of foxes and other wild mammals with dogs. The relevant Bill was enacted without the House of Lords' consent, in reliance on the Parliament Acts 1911 and 1949.

Jackson, who was a member of the Countryside Alliance, a group supportive of fox hunting, wished to challenge the validity of the Hunting Act.

In order to do so, he claimed that the 1949 Act – which had itself been passed without the Lords' consent under the 1911 Act – in effect involved the House of Commons using delegated legislation under the 1911 Act to enlarge its own powers, and that this was unlawful. He therefore contended that the 1949 Act and any legislation made under it (including the Hunting Act) was invalid.

Principle:

The House of Lords held that the Parliament Act 1949 is valid.

The 1911 Act created a new method of enacting primary legislation, with which the 1949 Act complied. The Hunting Act was therefore validly enacted under the 1949 Act.

In Chapter 6 we will examine the implications of this case for Parliamentary sovereignty.

SCRUTINY OF DELEGATED LEGISLATION

As society becomes more complex and highly regulated, law is increasingly being made by delegated legislation – i.e. by Government Ministers under powers granted ('delegated') to them by Act of Parliament.

While primary legislation sets out the 'framework' or principles within which delegated legislation must be made, the delegated legislation contains important details.

Parliament does not have time to scrutinise all delegated legislation fully. Most delegated legislation is made in the form of statutory instruments (SIs). The parent Act will specify whether or not delegated legislation made under it is subject to either of the following procedures under the **Statutory Instruments Act 1946**.

Negative procedure

Most SIs are subject to negative procedure, i.e. they are laid before Parliament for 40 days from the date they come into force, during which period Parliament can vote to annul the SI. It is extremely rare for Parliament to do so.

Affirmative procedure

Important SIs may require a positive vote in one or both Houses to bring them into effect. Parliament cannot amend delegated legislation – its only option is to accept it or reject it outright. In practice, the Joint Committee on Statutory Instruments acts as a check, and alerts Parliament if there are legal or technical problems.

The validity of delegated legislation can be challenged in the courts by judicial review (see Chapter 8).

The House of Lords and delegated legislation: the Strathclyde Review

In October 2015, the Government's proposals to cut tax credits were defeated in the House of Lords, leading to the abandonment of the policy. As the proposals were contained in a statutory instrument (rather than in primary legislation), neither the Salisbury Convention nor the Parliament Acts were engaged, but it is rare for the House of Lords to veto secondary legislation in this way.

The Conservative Government expressed frustration that the unelected House of Lords (in which the Conservatives did not have a majority) blocked a financial measure approved by the House of Commons, and commissioned a review of the House of Lords' powers to block secondary legislation, led by Lord Strathclyde. The report was published in December 2015 (see **Further reading**) and concludes that the House of Lords should not have the power to veto, but should be entitled to ask the Commons to reconsider, secondary legislation. The Government has undertaken to respond to the report in early 2016.

PARLIAMENT'S FUNCTIONS: SCRUTINISING THE GOVERNMENT

The relationship between Parliament and the Government will be examined in detail in Chapter 7. For now, the important point to note is that the Government is appointed almost exclusively from the political party (or parties) that has a controlling majority in the House of Commons.

This means that while Government Ministers are answerable to Parliament for the conduct of their departments, e.g. by having to answer questions about their work in the House of Commons, ultimately they can escape censure so long as they retain the support of their party colleagues. Parliament's ultimate sanction is to pass a motion of **no confidence**, following which the Government must resign and a General Election is called. However, given that the Government usually commands the support of a majority of the MPs in the Commons, it is unusual for it to lose a no-confidence vote so long as those MPs remain loyal to the party leadership.

This means that the theoretical control that Parliament has over the Government is somewhat undermined by the composition and party political balance of the Commons, which we will now analyse in detail.

THE HOUSE OF COMMONS

Membership

The House of Commons is a representative body. Its members are known as 'MPs' – Members of Parliament. They are elected by the public in a **General Election** (see below). There are 650 MPs in the House of Commons, each representing a different area of the UK (a 'constituency').

Constituencies vary significantly in their geographical size – some are large, sparsely populated rural areas; others are densely populated inner-city areas. The size of the electorate (number of voters) in each constituency is more consistent, averaging around 70,000 people.

General Elections (and by-elections)

A General Election is a national event in which, on the same day, a vote is held to elect a single MP in each one of the UK's 650 constituencies. Each person ('constituent') eligible to cast a vote in a constituency selects one candidate to be their MP from a list of candidates on a ballot paper. The candidate who gets the most votes in each constituency becomes the MP for that constituency and takes up a seat in the House of Commons until the next election. This is known as the '**first past the post**' system, and is controversial – see the discussion later on in this chapter.

A General Election used to occur when a Parliament was 'dissolved' by the Queen – by convention, at the request of the Prime Minister. This favoured the party currently in Government, which chose the most politically advantageous time for a General Election. The **Fixed-term Parliaments Act 2011** addresses this unfairness by fixing the dates of General Elections at five-yearly intervals from 7 May 2015. The Bill permits an early election (i.e. before the expiry of the five-year term) to be held if the House is unable to form a new Government after a vote of **no confidence** (see Chapter 7) or if at least two-thirds of the House vote in favour of an early election.

A **by-election** occurs when a vacancy in an individual constituency arises between General Elections, e.g. through the death of an MP. Sometimes a by-election is triggered when an MP decides to defect to another party (e.g. following the defections of Douglas Carswell MP and Mark Reckless MP from the Conservative Party to the UK Independence Party (UKIP) in 2014), although this is not legally required.

Political representation

Understanding the role of political parties is essential to understanding how democratic and how effective the House of Commons really is.

Of the 650 MPs currently in the House of Commons, all except four (and the **Speaker** – see below) belong to a legally recognised political party under the **Registration of Political Parties Act 1998.** The two main political parties (Labour and the Conservatives) hold 86 per cent of the seats between them. The Conservatives currently hold a majority of the 650 seats (330 seats, i.e. 50.8 per cent) and so they form the Government.

Parties play a crucial role in the electoral process, selecting candidates to stand for election and formulating the policies (contained in a 'manifesto') which the selected candidate is expected to support if elected. As each party can field only one candidate in each constituency, competition to stand as a leading party's candidate is fierce.

Once elected to the House of Commons, MPs are expected to vote in line with the leader of the party under whose manifesto they stood for election. The parties have developed a 'whip' system designed to enforce this expectation. MPs are not legally required to vote in line with the whip, but there are strong political incentives for members of the majority party to conform. MPs who defy their party leader are regarded as disloyal. They are very unlikely to be promoted to a senior position within the party, and those who regularly rebel may even be deselected from candidacy at the next General Election or expelled from the party.

> The real ambition of members of the legislature is to join the executive... they want to be promoted at best and re-elected at worst.
>
> Tony Wright MP, *British Politics: A Very Short Introduction*, 2003

First past the post

The results of the May 2015 General Election raised issues about the 'first past the post' voting system by which MPs are elected. Some people think that the system is unfair on, for example, UKIP, which secured 13 per cent of the vote, but only one seat in the House of Commons. UKIP polled 5 per cent more of the vote, but won 7 fewer seats than the Liberal Democrats, and polled 4 per cent more of the vote, but won 53 fewer seats than the Scottish National Party.

Results of May 2015 General Election			
Party	No. of seats in Commons	% of votes cast	% of seats won
Conservatives	330	37	51
Labour	231	31	36
Scottish National Party	54	5	9
Liberal Democrats	8	8	1
UKIP	1	13	0.2
Others	26	6	3.8

This happens because under the first past the post system, in order to win a seat in the Commons, an MP only has to get one more vote than the next most popular candidate in their constituency. For example, in 2015, Byron Davies (Conservative) was elected MP for the Gower constituency with 37.1 per cent of the votes cast in that constituency. Liz Evans (Labour) was the runner-up, with 37.0 per cent of the votes. The winning margin was just 27 votes. It is theoretically possible (although unlikely!) that if that pattern of voting were repeated in every constituency in the UK, the Conservatives would win every seat in the House of Commons and Labour would win none, even though they would have polled 37.0 per cent of the votes (and only 0.1 per cent less than the Conservatives).

Supporters of first past the vote argue that the system is simple to use and to count, and tends to be decisive, in that it usually produces a Government with a strong majority in the House of Commons – although it did not in 2010, when no single party won a majority of seats, and post-election negotiations produced a governing coalition of the Conservative and Liberal Democrat parties.

Opponents of first past the post argue that it is undemocratic at both the local and national levels. A total of 331 of the 650 MPs were elected on less than 50 per cent of the votes cast in their constituency in 2010 – so more than half of the voting public voted against them, and are arguably left unrepresented, with their votes 'wasted'. In some constituencies, people vote for candidates who they do not really support in order to try to remove the current MP, e.g. a Labour supporter living in a safe Conservative seat might vote Liberal Democrat, as she thinks that Labour have no chance of winning there, but wants the Conservatives out. This is known as 'tactical voting'.

At a national level, the number of seats won by the parties is disproportionate to their share of the actual votes cast. Traditionally, smaller parties have suffered the most from this disparity – e.g. in 2015, the Green Party won 1.1 million votes, comprising 3.8 per cent of the overall votes cast, but won just one seat in the Commons. As detailed above, however, the biggest victims of the current system were UKIP, which polled 13 per cent of the vote, but also won just one seat. This is because support for UKIP was spread relatively evenly throughout the UK rather than being concentrated in particular constituencies.

Proportional representation

Parties such as UKIP and the Green Party have called for electoral reform to a system of **proportional representation**, in which the number of seats allocated to a party reflects their share of the overall vote.

In a May 2011 referendum, the electorate decisively rejected a proposal to adopt the **Alternative Vote** system, a form of proportional representation in which voters rank each candidate in their constituency in order of preference. Anyone getting more than 50 per cent in the first round is elected, otherwise the candidate with the fewest votes is eliminated and their backers' second choices are allocated to those remaining. This process continues until a winner (i.e. someone getting more than 50 per cent) emerges.

This system is argued by its supporters to be more representative, i.e. to better reflect the wishes of the electorate, than the first past the post system. It is not, however, without its critics – some people think that it militates against a strong, stable Government, while others think it does not go far enough in terms of achieving **proportional representation**, i.e. ensuring that smaller parties get a fairer share of the seats in the House of Commons.

Government and opposition

It is important to remember that there is a difference in function between Parliament and Government. The Government runs the country; the role of Parliament is to set the legal limits within which the Government can do this.

There, is however, an overlap of personnel. By convention, the person who commands the support of a majority of MPs in the House of Commons is appointed by the Queen as

Prime Minister (PM). This is usually the leader of the political party which won the most seats at a general election. The PM is invited by the Queen to form a Government. The PM does this by choosing Ministers (by convention, the Queen appoints whoever the PM chooses), who are responsible for running Government Departments, proposing new laws and implementing the laws enacted by Parliament.

Section 2 of the House of Commons Disqualification Act 1975 limits the number of Government Ministers in the House of Commons to 95, but they are supported by a raft of unpaid sub-ministerial posts (e.g. Parliamentary Private Secretaries) so that a significant proportion of the MPs belonging to the party with the most seats in the Commons are also members of the Government.

This overlap, combined with the strength of the main political parties, has profound implications for the effectiveness of the House of Commons in performing its main functions of scrutinising and enacting legislation, and holding the Government to account. Those MPs who belong to a governing party, but who have not themselves been given jobs in the Government, sit in Parliament purely as legislators and are known as 'backbenchers'. They are expected to support the Government in debates and votes on legislation, otherwise they risk losing out on promotion or, worse still, deselection.

The remaining MPs in the House of Commons belong to the other parties. The next largest party outside the Government is known as the official Opposition which has a Leader and Shadow Ministers of its own – in theory, a 'Government in waiting'. Their job is to use Parliament as a forum to challenge the Government on its legislative proposals and its actions. Again, opposition MPs are subject to the party whips and tend to support their leader's stance for reasons of political solidarity, ambition and self-preservation.

This partisan approach tends to make voting in the Commons predictable, with few MPs being persuaded to go against the whips, and the Government usually getting its way.

Speaker

The Speaker presides over debates and voting in the House of Commons, acting as a 'chair'. The Speaker must remain politically impartial at all times and must maintain order by ensuring that MPs conform to the House of Commons' own internal rules of procedure, and that all MPs who wish to speak get a fair chance to do so.

On-the-spot question

How 'democratic' do you consider the House of Commons to be?

THE HOUSE OF LORDS

The House of Lords is referred to as 'the second chamber' – to reflect its political and legal subordinacy to the democratically elected Commons (see above). Members of the House of Lords are not elected by the general public, but are appointed by a variety of means.

Membership

There is no limit on the membership of the House of Lords – there are currently around 820 members, made up of three different types:

Hereditary peers (92)

Until the **House of Lords Act 1999**, the majority of the Lords (at that time, about 1,350!) were hereditary peers, i.e. those who had inherited titles bestowed by the monarch on their ancestors.

The **House of Lords Act 1999** removed all bar 92 hereditary peers. When one of these hereditary peers dies, they are replaced by a by-election among the remaining hereditary peers in the political group to which the deceased member belonged.

Lords spiritual (26)

Twenty-six senior clergy of the Church of England sit in the House of Lords. They are chosen by the Queen (on the PM's advice) from a list of nominations provided by the Church. They are members of the House until they retire as bishops, etc. Dignitaries from other faiths are not eligible within this category, but can be appointed to the House of Lords as ordinary life peers.

Life peers (around 700)

The Queen formally appoints life peers, but by convention does so on the advice and recommendation of the PM. These Lords are appointed for their lifetime only – their title does not pass to their children.

The life peers nominated by the PM are generally chosen from lists submitted by the main political parties. They are subject to vetting by a non-statutory House of Lords Appointments Commission (but its decisions are not binding). This Commission also makes its own non-political nominations for appointments as life peers direct to the Queen.

In 2006 and 2007, the police conducted a criminal investigation into the alleged sale of life peerages in return for contributions to political parties under the **Honours (Prevention of Abuses) Act 1925**. No charges were brought.

Note: Until 2009, there used to be a fourth type of member of the House of Lords – the **Law Lords**. These were 12 judges (who were also life peers) specifically appointed because of their legal expertise to hear appeals from the Court of Appeal and lower courts. The **Constitutional Reform Act 2005**, which came into force on 1 October 2009, removed the Law Lords from the House, and their functions are now exercised by the judges of the new, separate **Supreme Court**: see Chapter 8. So the House of Lords no longer has a judicial function – its functions are purely legislative.

This change was necessary to achieve a proper separation of powers between the legislature and the judiciary, and to comply with Article 6 of the European Convention on Human Rights, which requires that disputes are determined by an independent tribunal. You will see references to cases decided by the House of Lords before 2009, but it is important to remember that the highest court in the UK is now the Supreme Court, and that the House of Lords no longer has a judicial role.

Political parties

The House of Lords currently contains around 148 'crossbench' (i.e. politically independent) members, 209 Labour members, 202 Conservative members and 107 Liberal Democrat members. As a result, voting in the House of Lords is more difficult to predict than in the House of Commons because no single party has a majority of members.

Overlap between the House of Lords and the Government

There are no legal limits (other than the limit on ministerial salaries in the **Ministerial and Other Salaries Act 1975**) to the number of Ministers who can be members of the House of Lords, but by convention Ministers heading major spending departments are drawn from the Commons.

Further reform of the House of Lords?

The (partial) exclusion of hereditary peers by the **House of Lords Act 1999** was intended to be the first stage of reform to the House. Further reform will require additional legislation, and has been the subject of much Government consultation and Parliamentary debate. The political parties, while generally agreeing that further reform is needed, have been unable to establish a consensus as to what form this should take. For example, in March 2007, the House of Commons voted in a debate on Lords reform for either an 80 per cent or a 100 per cent *elected* second chamber. A week later, the Lords voted for a 100 per cent *appointed* chamber.

The House of Lords Reform Act 2014 provides for the resignation of members, and for the exclusion of any peer convicted of a criminal offence and sentenced to a term of imprisonment of one year or more.

The most recent attempt to fundamentally reform the composition of the House was the coalition Government's **House of Lords Reform Bill**, which was introduced into the House of Commons in June 2012. In summary, the Bill proposed to:

- retain the name 'House of Lords';
- reduce it to 450 members, 80 per cent of whom are to be elected and 20 per cent to be appointed;
- use a proportionate 'open list' system to elect 360 members (with 120 members to be elected every five years from May 2015);
- create a statutory Appointments Commission to recommend 60 members to be appointed by the Queen;
- limit both elected and appointed members to single, non-renewable 15-year terms of office;
- allow 12 Bishops of the Church of England to sit as *ex officio* members;
- retain the primacy of the House of Commons and not change the constitutional powers of the House of Lords.

The Bill was abandoned in August 2012 once it became clear that it lacked sufficient political support within Parliament to be enacted. It remains to be seen whether the Government's response to the Strathclyde Review (referred to above and referenced in your **Further reading** for this chapter) will re-open the question of fundamental reform of the House of Lords' role and composition.

On-the-spot questions

In a modern democracy it is important that those who make the laws of the land should be elected by those to whom those laws apply. The House of Lords performs its work well but lacks sufficient democratic authority.

David Cameron and Nick Clegg, 'Foreword', House of Lords Reform Draft Bill, May 2011

Do you agree that 'the House of Lords performs its work well but lacks sufficient authority'? Would the proposals in the House of Lords Reform Bill have improved Parliament as a whole? How might they have affected relations between the two Houses? Do you think that it is time to fundamentally reconsider the role and composition of the House of Lords?

THE QUEEN'S ROLE IN PARLIAMENT

The Queen exercises important legal powers within Parliament. They include:

- granting Royal Assent to legislation which has passed through both Houses of Parliament, giving the Queen the final say on whether proposed legislation becomes law;
- 'proroguing' (closing) Parliament at the end of a Parliamentary session and re-opening it again for the next session;
- appointing the PM and other Ministers.

In practice, the Queen's exercise of these powers is governed by convention. The Queen appoints as PM the person who she thinks can command the support of a majority of MPs in the House of Commons. Usually, this will be the leader of the political party which holds a majority of seats following a General Election, although where no single party holds such a majority (such as after the 2010 General Election), the Queen may wait to see whether negotiations between the parties produce a coalition (an alliance of parties) which, together, commands sufficient support in the House of Commons to be able to govern effectively.

By convention, the Queen then exercises the other legal powers set out above on her PM's advice so that her role is largely formal and ceremonial. This does not mean, however, that it is unimportant. The Queen has the opportunity, via private weekly meetings with the Prime Minister (see Chapter 7), to influence Government, and the fact that, as a matter of law, the ultimate power to decide whether or not a particular Bill becomes law resides with the Queen is seen as a constitutional long-stop to safeguard against the abuse of political power.

The courts have consistently ruled that conventions are not legally binding (see, for example, the case of *Attorney General v Jonathan Cape* **(1975) 3 WLR 606, QBD** in Chapter 7), and in light of the oath of allegiance sworn by judges to the Queen, one has to assume that the courts would uphold a decision by the Queen to refuse Royal Assent to a particular Bill. No monarch, however, has refused Royal Assent since the Scottish Militia Bill of 1707, and were the Queen to do so, this could precipitate a constitutional crisis. It would politicise the monarchy and call into question the right of the unelected monarch to frustrate the will of Parliament.

On the other hand, some commentators consider that the fact that the Queen has such a power (and that its exercise would lead to a constitutional crisis) has a benign influence on proposals for legislation, since the requirement to obtain Royal Assent acts as a deterrent to political parties from exploiting a large majority in the House of Commons to enact legislation which curtails fundamental rights or which alters the constitution for the party's own benefit.

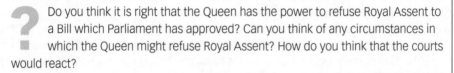

On-the-spot questions

Do you think it is right that the Queen has the power to refuse Royal Assent to a Bill which Parliament has approved? Can you think of any circumstances in which the Queen might refuse Royal Assent? How do you think that the courts would react?

SUMMARY

- Parliament's role is to make laws (legislate), examine the work of Government (scrutinise) and raise taxes.
- It comprises the elected House of Commons, the unelected House of Lords and the Queen. The composition of the two Houses, and the relationship between them, has evolved over centuries of social and political change, rather than as the result of a codified constitution.
- The House of Commons has primacy within Parliament. Legally, this is due to the Parliament Acts 1911 and 1949. Politically, it is because MPs are elected and therefore the Commons claims democratic legitimacy. There are questions, however, about whether the first past the post electoral system used to elect MPs is truly representative of the electorate.
- There is a lack of political consensus about whether the House of Lords should be reformed and, if so, how. The most recent failed attempt is the House of Lords Reform Bill, which would have created a House of 450 members, with 80 per cent elected using a proportionate 'open list' voting system. The Bill was abandoned in August 2012 due to lack of political support. The role of the Lords, and its relationship with the Commons, is currently being considered in the context of the Strathclyde Review.

FURTHER READING

Adams, T, 'Royal consent and hidden power', UK Constitutional Law Blog (26 January 2013), available at http://ukconstitutionallaw.org – an article about the symbolic and real power of the monarchy in Parliament.

Reid, P, '"English votes on English law": Just another running repair', UK Constitutional Law Blog (28 October 2015), available at http://ukconstitutionallaw.org – a more in-depth piece on the legal and practical difficulties arising from EVEL.

http://ohrh.law.ox.ac.uk/prisoner-voting-and-the-rule-of-law-the-irony-of-non-compliance – a short piece written in 2013 by John Hirst, the complainant in **Hirst v UK (2005)**, about the continuing failure of the UK Government to implement the European Court of Human Rights' ruling.

www.parliament.uk/briefing-papers/SN01764.pdf – *Prisoners' Voting Rights*, a House of Commons library research paper providing a narrative of events following the decision In **Hirst (2005)**. It refers to statements by the Prime Minister, David Cameron, setting out his absolute opposition to granting the vote to prisoners.

www.parliament.uk/about/podcasts/theworkofparliament/select-committees-in-the-house-of-commons/why-are-select-committees-important – a short film on the UK Parliament's website explaining the importance of Select Committees.

www.instituteforgovernment.org.uk/sites/default/files/publications/Under%20scrutiny%20final.pdf – the Institute for Government's report into the operation of Select Committees in the 2010–15 Parliament. Detailed, but contains an excellent section at pages 20–26 on 'Eight lessons about impact from scrutiny'.

www.independent.co.uk/voices/evel-isnt-about-scotland-its-about-locking-labour-out-of-power-in-the-uk-a6706701.html – an editorial piece in *The Independent* newspaper, arguing that EVEL is 'the most narrow-minded exercise in partisan constitutionalism in British history'.

www.electoral-reform.org.uk/file/1767/download?token=cY4ruQ3t – the Electoral Reform Society's report, *The 2015 General Election: A Voting System in Crisis*, argues that the 2015 General Election result is the most disproportionate result In UK election history.

www.consoc.org.uk/category/house-of-lords – an article examining the failure of the House of Lords Reform Bill and criticising the main political parties' piecemeal approach to constitutional reform.

www.gov.uk/government/publications/strathclyde-review-secondary-legislation-and-the-primacy-of-the-house-of-commons – *Strathclyde Review: Secondary Legislation and the Primacy of the House of Commons*, 17 December 2015.

www.theguardian.com/commentisfree/2015/dec/13/the-guardian-view-on-the-strathclyde-review-of-the-lords-beware-a-government-power-grab – an editorial piece in *The Guardian*, arguing that the question of the House of Lords' powers should be considered alongside its composition.

www.parliament.uk – contains information about the membership and procedures of the Houses of Commons and Lords, and a bill tracker enabling you to check the progress of legislation.

COMPANION WEBSITE

An online glossary compiled by the author is available on the companion website: www.routledge.com/cw/beginningthelaw

Chapter 6
Parliamentary sovereignty

LEARNING OBJECTIVES

After reading this chapter, you should be able to:

- Define what is meant by Parliamentary sovereignty
- Refer to cases in which the courts have accepted Parliament's legislative supremacy
- Explain the impact of European Union (EU) membership on Parliamentary sovereignty
- Contrast this with the more limited impact of the Human Rights Act 1998 (HRA 1998)
- Discuss whether Parliament could entrench a constitutional statute.

INTRODUCTION

As we saw in Chapters 2 and 3, the UK has an uncodified constitution comprised of a variety of written, legal sources (legislation and case law) and non-written, political sources (conventions).

The central principle around which the UK constitution has evolved is the doctrine of Parliamentary sovereignty. It is a legal, common law rule by which the courts recognise Acts of Parliament as the highest law of the land – contrast this with the USA, where Acts of Congress may be declared invalid by the US Supreme Court if they violate the US Constitution.

This chapter will define Parliamentary sovereignty, examine its development by the courts and then consider recent challenges to the traditional doctrine arising at both a domestic and an international level.

WHAT IS SOVEREIGNTY?

As with so much of constitutional law, it is important to be aware that Parliamentary sovereignty has both legal and political meanings. While as lawyers, we are primarily concerned with Parliamentary sovereignty as a legal rule, you will see throughout this chapter that the case law and jurisprudence from which the rule derives cannot be isolated from its political context. In order to write a good essay on this topic, you therefore need to be able to discuss Parliamentary sovereignty from both a legal and a political perspective.

Legally, Parliamentary sovereignty describes the relationship between the legislature and the judiciary, which has traditionally been one in which the UK's courts recognise Parliament as the supreme law-maker and unquestioningly apply its Acts (though, as we will see below, there are signs that this relationship may be changing).

Politically, sovereignty has different shades of meaning. It refers partly to the independence of the UK from other nation States, and its ability to determine its own economic, political and legal affairs without foreign interference. But it also refers to the idea that, in a democracy, ultimate sovereignty resides with the electorate, on whose votes MPs depend for office and on whose co-operation they depend for the effectiveness of the laws they enact.

There are many competing definitions of Parliamentary sovereignty, but the one you are most likely to come across in lectures, coursework and examinations is Dicey's:

Key Definition

Parliamentary sovereignty: 'Parliamentary sovereignty means neither more nor less than this, namely that Parliament has, under the English constitution, the right to make or unmake any law whatever; and further that no person or body is recognised by the law of England as having a right to override or set aside the legislation of Parliament.'

A V Dicey, *Introduction to the Study of the Law of the Constitution* (1885)

WHAT DOES DICEY'S DEFINITION OF PARLIAMENTARY SOVEREIGNTY MEAN?

Dicey's definition of sovereignty can be translated into three principles:

	Dicey's definition	Principle
1	'the right to make… any law'	Parliament can make any law on any subject – it has unlimited legislative competence
2	'the right to… unmake any law'	Parliament can change or repeal laws passed by earlier Parliaments – so Parliament cannot restrict its successors (i.e. future Parliaments)
3	'no person or body [can] … override or set aside the legislation of Parliament'	Acts of Parliament are the highest form of law – their validity cannot be challenged

We will now examine the legal authorities supporting each principle of Dicey's definition of Parliamentary sovereignty, before we investigate recent legal and political limitations on the doctrine, in particular:

- devolution to Scotland and Wales;
- membership of the EU and EU law;
- HRA 1998;
- a developing concept of 'constitutional' statutes and of potential common law limitations on Parliamentary sovereignty in the courts;
- the courts' recognition that Parliament can 'redefine' the way it enacts legislation.

PARLIAMENT'S LEGISLATIVE COMPETENCE

There is a succession of key cases in which the courts have dismissed challenges to the *content* of Acts of Parliament on the basis that Parliament has unlimited legislative competence. If you can cite some of these cases in examinations and coursework, they will add authority to your answer:

Case	Summary	Quote	Principle
Cheney v Conn (1968) 1 All ER 779, HC	C refused to pay taxes imposed by the Finance Act 1964 on the basis that they would be spent on nuclear weapons, contrary to the Geneva Convention. The courts held that the Act was lawful and that the tax must be paid.	'What the statute itself enacts cannot be unlawful, because what the statute says and provides is itself the law, and the highest form of law that is known to this country.'	Statute overrides international law.
Madzimbamuto v Lardner-Burke (1969) 1 AC 645, HL	In spite of the unilateral declaration of independence in Southern Rhodesia, Parliament enacted the Southern Rhodesia Act 1965, breaching the convention that the UK would not legislate for that country without the consent of its Parliament. The UK courts upheld the Act's validity.	'It is often said that it would be unconstitutional for the United Kingdom Parliament to do certain things, meaning that the moral, political and other reasons against doing them are so strong that most people would regard [them] as highly improper… But that does not mean that it is beyond the power of Parliament… the courts could not hold the Act of Parliament invalid.'	Statute overrides convention.

(Continued)

Case	Summary	Quote	Principle
Burmah Oil Co v Lord Advocate (1965) AC 75, HL	The House of Lords held that Burmah Oil was entitled to compensation for the destruction of its oil installations by the British Government during World War II. In response to that ruling, Parliament enacted the **War Damage Act 1965** providing that no compensation was payable for past or future acts of destruction committed by the Government in the national interest during a time of war.		Statute can operate retrospectively. Statute overrides common law. Statute extinguishes prerogative powers (see Chapter 7).

These cases, particularly *Burmah Oil Co v Lord Advocate* (1965), demonstrate the courts' traditional reluctance to question Acts of Parliament, even where the content of the Act arguably offends the principles of good law-making. As you will see later in this chapter, however, when you learn about the case of *AXA v Lord Advocate* (2011) UKSC 46, the Supreme Court has recently suggested that there may be limits to the doctrine and that where an Act of Parliament goes 'beyond the pale', the Court may be prepared to intervene.

NO-ONE CAN CHALLENGE THE VALIDITY OF AN ACT OF PARLIAMENT

The courts have also been unwilling to entertain challenges to the procedure by which an Act is passed. Their reasoning derives from **Article 9 of the Bill of Rights 1689**, which provides that 'the freedom of speech and debates or proceedings in Parliament ought not to be impeached or questioned in any court or place out of Parliament'. In effect, the courts have taken the view that Parliament is self-regulating, at least so far as the enactment of legislation is concerned.

In *Pickin v British Railways Board* (1974) AC 765, HL, the House of Lords refused to consider a technical challenge to the procedure by which Parliament had enacted a private Act, the effect of which was to deprive the challenger of his land. This is known as the **enrolled Act rule**, i.e. that the courts will not inquire into the validity of an Act of Parliament which states that it has been properly enacted.

PARLIAMENT CANNOT LIMIT FUTURE PARLIAMENTS

This is the most difficult aspect of Dicey's definition of Parliamentary sovereignty. Arguably, it contradicts Dicey's assertion that Parliament's legislative competence is unlimited: if Parliament can really make any law whatsoever, can it not make laws about the procedure by which Parliament changes or repeals certain Acts?

This question is very important, because if Parliament cannot impose procedural restrictions on future Parliaments in this way, then it would seem impossible for the UK to entrench constitutional laws like the USA has (see Chapter 2).

The traditional theory of 'continuing' Parliamentary sovereignty requires that, after each General Election, Parliament should be free to pass new legislation on any subject-matter and to amend or repeal any legislation enacted by a previous Parliament. The reason behind this is that Parliament (or at least the House of Commons!) has been elected by the people in accordance with the political mood of the age, and that it should therefore be free to make and change the law in order to reflect this. The courts have developed the principle of **implied repeal** to give effect to this democratic mandate.

It is important for assessment questions on Parliamentary sovereignty that you can explain the implied repeal rule and distinguish it from express repeal of Acts of Parliament:

Key Definitions

Express repeal: Where a later statute expressly (i.e. by the plain words of the Act itself) repeals an earlier one and replaces it with new provisions, the courts will give effect to those new provisions (e.g. the **Government of Wales Act 2006** repeals and replaces most of the Government of Wales Act 1998). This is simply a case of obeying the direction given by Parliament in the Act.

Implied repeal: Where a later statute conflicts with an earlier statute which it does not expressly repeal, the courts apply the later statute in preference to the earlier one, which they deem to be impliedly repealed. This is a common law doctrine developed by the courts to give effect to the constitutional principle that Parliament cannot bind its successors.

For example, in *Ellen Street Estates v Minister for Health* (1934) 1 KB 590, CA, the Housing Act 1925 provided for a less generous compensation scheme for the compulsory acquisition of land than an unrepealed Act passed in 1919. The Court of Appeal applied the 1925 Act, even though the 1919 Act contained a provision that any later inconsistent scheme 'shall not have effect'. Lord Justice Maugham rejected this apparent attempt to entrench the 1919 Act:

> The legislature cannot, according to our constitution, bind itself as to the form of subsequent legislation and it is impossible for Parliament to enact that in a subsequent statute dealing with the same subject-matter there can be no implied repeal.

The *Ellen Street Estates* (1934) case can perhaps be seen as the high-water mark of Parliamentary sovereignty, demonstrating an absolute unwillingness on the part of the judges to allow Parliament to restrict itself.

It is important to realise, however, that the doctrine of implied repeal is a common law rule (as is the doctrine of Parliamentary sovereignty itself). It was created by the judges and can therefore be changed by the judges.

Recent case law, which we will now assess, suggests that the doctrine is indeed being developed to reflect a new dynamic between the courts and Parliament. These cases are best understood in the context of an examination of recent constitutional developments which arguably threaten, to a greater or lesser extent, the contemporary relevance and accuracy of Dicey's definition of Parliamentary sovereignty. When answering essay questions on this topic, you can refer to the authorities discussed below as evidence for or against this argument.

TRANSFER OF LAW-MAKING POWERS TO SCOTLAND, WALES AND NORTHERN IRELAND

Following the Labour Party's victory in the 1997 General Election, significant legislative power was devolved (i.e. granted via Acts of Parliament) by the UK Parliament to newly created legislatures in Scotland, Wales and Northern Ireland.

The scheme of devolution differs in each case.

Scotland Act 1998

A 1997 referendum on devolution to Scotland resulted in a 74 per cent 'yes' vote. As a result, the UK Parliament enacted the Scotland Act 1998, creating both a Scottish Parliament and the Scottish Executive (a national Government for Scotland).

The 1998 Act gives the Scottish Parliament power to make primary legislation for Scotland (Acts of the Scottish Parliament) in *any area except* those powers which the 1998 Act specifically reserves to the UK Parliament (e.g. foreign policy and national security). So, for example, the Scottish Parliament can pass an Act to authorise taxation in Scotland. The default position is that, unless the 1998 Act expressly reserves the matter to the UK Parliament, the Scottish Parliament can legislate about it. This is known as a 'reserved powers model' of devolution.

In September 2014, the Scottish people voted in a referendum for Scotland to remain in the UK by a margin of 55 per cent to 45 per cent. The Scottish National Party (SNP), which supported the vote for Scotland to leave the UK and become an independent country, remains the largest party in the Scottish Parliament, forms the Scottish Government (the executive) and continues to support Scottish independence.

Some of the other potential constitutional reforms discussed in this chapter and in Chapter 11 could have important consequences for the future of the UK. For example, the SNP has said that it wants Scotland to continue to be a member of the EU, so if the UK decides to leave the EU, this could prompt a call for another referendum on Scottish independence. The SNP has also expressed opposition to proposals by the UK Government to repeal HRA 1998, which is hard-wired into the Scottish devolution settlement by the Scotland Act 1998.

Government of Wales Acts 1998 and 2006

As the 1997 referendum on Welsh devolution resulted in a 'yes' vote of only 50.3 per cent, the initial scheme of devolution to Wales was a much more 'watered-down' version than the Scotland Act 1998. The Government of Wales Act 1998 created a single body (the National Assembly for Wales), with no formal separation between the legislature (the Assembly) and the executive (unofficially the 'Welsh Assembly Government', although there was no such body in law). These arrangements proved impractical and out of date almost as soon as they were made.

The 1998 Act was largely repealed and replaced by the Government of Wales Act 2006, which provided for the formal separation of the Assembly and the Welsh Government, and for the incremental transfer of further powers to Wales (reflecting the comment of the former Secretary of State for Wales, Ron Davies MP, that 'devolution is a process, not an event'). Following a 2011 referendum approving the further transfer of powers to Wales under the 2006 Act, the Assembly is now able to enact primary legislation for Wales which relates to any of the 20 subjects listed in Schedule 7 to that Act (e.g. education, economic development and health), and does not fall within the exceptions set out in that Schedule. There are significant policy areas in which the Assembly cannot legislate, e.g. policing and criminal justice, foreign affairs and defence and social security. The power to make laws for Wales in relation to these areas remains with the UK Parliament.

This settlement is known as a 'conferred powers' model, in which the default position is that the Assembly *cannot* legislate about a matter unless the 2006 Act says that it can. This may be contrasted with the Scottish reserved powers model. Following calls from the Welsh Government to move to a reserved powers model of devolution, the UK Government published a draft Wales Bill in October 2015 which, if enacted, will achieve this. At the time of writing, negotiations about the draft Wales Bill are continuing between the Welsh and UK Governments.

Northern Ireland Acts 1998 and 2000

The 1998 Act established a devolved legislative Assembly for Northern Ireland and a power-sharing executive body statutorily required to comprise members of political parties broadly representing both the predominantly Protestant, unionist community (who favoured remaining in the UK) and the predominantly Roman Catholic, republican community (who favoured independence). This unique settlement reflected the troubled history of Northern Ireland, which had endured sustained violent clashes between these two communities over the previous 30 years. The Assembly is empowered to make primary legislation on any matter which the 1998 Act does not expressly except from its competence or reserve to the UK Parliament.

In 2002, powers devolved to the Northern Ireland Assembly were recalled to Westminster under the Northern Ireland Act 2000, following serious disagreements between the main Northern Irish political parties and the withdrawal of the unionist parties from the Assembly. The Northern Ireland (St Andrews Agreement) Act 2006 provided for the re-devolution of power to the Assembly, subject to certain detailed conditions.

What about England-only matters?

Now that law-making powers in certain policy areas have been devolved to Scotland, Wales and Northern Ireland, the UK Parliament increasingly finds itself, in those areas, legislating only for England.

You read in Chapter 5 about how one of the consequences of Parliament devolving additional powers to Scotland has been that the House of Commons has changed its Standing Orders to require that Bill provisions whose effect is confined to England (or England and Wales) require the consent of a majority of English (or English and Welsh) MPs before the Bill can become law; this is known as English votes for English laws (EVEL).

When you have finished reading this chapter, you might find it helpful to think further about the on-the-spot question about EVEL in Chapter 5. Given that, as you will see below, the UK Parliament retains ultimate power to legislate for Scotland, Wales and Northern Ireland, is it democratic, or constitutionally logical, for the UK Parliament to deal with English matters in this way?

DEVOLUTION – A LEGAL LIMIT OR A POLITICAL LIMIT?

The question here is whether the UK Parliament could undo the effects of devolution and reclaim those powers which it voluntarily transferred to the devolved legislatures.

As a matter of law, the UK Parliament could repeal any of the above Acts and therefore dissolve the legal basis upon which the devolved institutions operate. The UK Parliament has also retained the express power in the above Acts to continue legislating for Scotland, Wales and Northern Ireland, even in relation to devolved matters. The Sewel Convention provides that Parliament will not normally do so without the devolved legislature's consent, but the Convention is not legally enforceable. At the time of writing, the UK Government is pressing ahead with the UK-wide Trade Union Bill, despite the National Assembly for Wales refusing to grant its consent for those provisions which affect public services in Wales.

On a purely legal analysis, therefore, ultimate power resides at Westminster and the sovereignty of the UK Parliament is to that extent not limited by devolution.

In reality, the constraints on the UK Parliament are political rather than legal. Lord Denning, commenting on grants of independence to former UK colonies in *Blackburn v Attorney General* (1971), said that:

> in legal theory, one Parliament cannot bind another, and… no Act is irreversible. But legal theory does not always march alongside political reality… Freedom once given cannot be taken away.

What Lord Denning meant is that, from a political perspective, Acts of devolution are usually irreversible. For example, given that the people of Scotland recently elected the SNP on a pro-independence manifesto, it is currently hard to imagine that the UK Parliament would, in defiance of the Scottish electorate, repeal the Scotland Act 1998 and dissolve the Scottish Parliament. To do so could risk civil disobedience, undermining the rule of law.

The suspension of the Northern Ireland Assembly from 2002 to 2007 does demonstrate, however, that powers conferred by devolution *can* be recalled by the UK Parliament where the political circumstances permit. While the Northern Ireland experience is exceptional, this episode does demonstrate that, ultimately, the limits imposed on Parliamentary supremacy by devolution are political rather than legal. Further, there have been suggestions from commentators on the draft Wales Bill that aspects of it represent an attempt by the UK Government to reclaim some powers devolved to Wales in the 2006 Act.

A recent Supreme Court case demonstrates the respect afforded by the courts to Acts of the devolved legislatures, while also raising the possibility that there may be some legal limits to the traditional doctrine of Parliamentary sovereignty:

KEY CASE: *AXA v Lord Advocate* **(2011) UKSC 46**

Background:

The Scottish Parliament enacted the Damages (Asbestos-Related Conditions) (Scotland) Act 2009, which provides that those suffering from pleural plaques caused by work-related exposure to asbestos could recover damages. In Scotland, this Act overturned a judicial decision of the House of Lords in the case of *Rothwell* [2007] UKHL 39 that pleural plaques were not an actionable personal injury. AXA, which insured employers, stood to be liable for significant payouts as a result of claims brought under the Act. It challenged the legality of the Act, both on the grounds that:

(1)   it was incompatible with Article 1 to Protocol 1 (A1P1) of the European Convention on Human Rights (see Chapter 9); and

(2)   it was an unreasonable, arbitrary and irrational exercise of the Scottish Parliament's power to legislate under the Scotland Act 1998, and could therefore be judicially reviewed (see Chapter 8).

Principle:

The Supreme Court held that:

(1)   while A1P1 was engaged, it had not been violated as the interference with the insurance companies' A1P1 rights was a proportionate means of achieving a legitimate aim (see Chapter 9); and

(2)   while Acts of the Scottish Parliament could in principle be judicially reviewed, they could not be reviewed on the grounds of unreasonableness, arbitrariness or irrationality.

The Act was therefore upheld. What is particularly interesting about the case is the reasoning adopted by Lord Hope, who gave the leading judgment. Lord Hope considered that the Scottish Parliament's democratic credentials, like those of the UK Parliament, meant that the courts could intervene to declare its legislation invalid only on exceptional grounds, e.g. where that legislation sought to abolish judicial review or to abrogate people's fundamental rights. Lord Hope said that:

Whether this is likely to happen is not the point. It is enough that it might conceivably do so. The rule of law requires that the judges must retain the power to insist that legislation of that extreme kind is not law that the courts will recognise.

Lord Hope made it clear that this part of his reasoning applied to the UK Parliament as much as to the Scottish Parliament. Since the case did not concern an Act of the UK Parliament, this part of the judgment is *obiter* (not binding on future courts), but it does suggest that there may be limits to what the courts will be prepared to accept under the doctrine of Parliamentary sovereignty.

On-the-spot question

When you have finished reading this chapter, consider why Lord Hope might have decided to say that there are limits on the laws that the UK Parliament can make. Can you think of examples of laws that Parliament might make, but that the Supreme Court might refuse to uphold?

MEMBERSHIP OF THE EUROPEAN UNION AND EU LAW

The EU is an economic and political union of 28 Member States, with the competence to legislate for those Member States in specific areas set out in the various EU treaties (e.g. in relation to the free movement of people, services and goods between Member States in order to create a single Europe-wide market). The UK joined the EU in 1973.

The legal instrument by which it did so is the **European Communities Act 1972 (ECA 1972)**, the key provisions of which are as follows:

	European Communities Act 1972
s 2(1)	gives legal effect in the UK to 'directly effective' EU law
s 2(4)	a statutory rule of interpretation which requires any past or future UK enactment (primary or secondary legislation) to 'be construed and have effect' subject to directly effective EU law
s 3(1)	requires UK courts to apply EU law in accordance with principles laid down by the Court of Justice of the European Union (CJEU)

The CJEU has consistently asserted the view that, in the event of a conflict between EU law and the national law of a Member State, the national court must apply EU law. For example, in *Costa v ENEL* [1964] (Case 6/64) [1964] ECR 1125, ECJ, it said:

The transfer by the states from their domestic legal system to the [EU] legal system... carries with it a permanent limitation of their sovereign rights.

This is a controversial topic – and therefore often used for assessment questions! The issues are the extent to which, by joining the EU, the UK has limited its 'sovereign rights' and the question of whether it has done so 'permanently'. You should be aware, in reading about this topic, that the UK Government has promised to hold a referendum on the question of whether the UK should remain in the EU in June 2016.

TO WHAT EXTENT DOES EU LAW LIMIT PARLIAMENTARY SOVEREIGNTY?

The UK courts take the view that, for so long as s 2(4) ECA 1972 remains unrepealed, they are bound by that provision to 'construe and [give] effect' to Acts of Parliament only to the extent that they are compatible with EU law. This means that where a provision in an Act of Parliament contradicts EU law, the courts must 'set it aside':

KEY CASE: *Factortame Ltd v Secretary of State (No 2)* [1991] 1 AC 603

Background:

The Merchant Shipping Act 1988 imposed restrictions on non-UK fishing vessels operating in British waters. A Spanish operator complained that the Act contravened directly effective provisions in the EU Treaty and that the restrictions would damage its business. It asked the House of Lords for an injunction to stop the Act coming into effect while it waited for a ruling from the CJEU on whether the Act was incompatible with the Treaty.

Initially, the House of Lords refused the injunction, but sought a ruling from the CJEU on whether it was obliged to 'suspend' the Act until the CJEU decided on compatibility.

Principle:

The CJEU held that the Act should be suspended and the House of Lords agreed to do so, granting the injunction.

Lord Bridge:

Some public comments... have suggested that this was a novel and dangerous invasion by a [European Union] institution of the sovereignty of the UK Parliament... whatever limitation the UK Parliament accepted when it enacted the European Communities Act 1972 was entirely voluntary.

Sir William Wade thought that the disapplication of an Act of Parliament by the courts in *Factortame* amounted to a 'constitutional revolution', in which the courts adapted the common law doctrine of continuing Parliamentary sovereignty to accommodate the 'political reality' that membership of the EU requires compliance with EU law. This may, however, be overstating the case. While *Factortame* is a landmark decision, it is not entirely incompatible with Dicey's doctrine, since although the House of Lords 'set aside' the Merchant Shipping Act 1988 (thereby contravening Dicey's third principle that 'no one… can override or set aside the legislation of Parliament'), the judges did so on the basis that they were required to do so by the rule in s 2(4) ECA 1972 – itself an Act of Parliament. In other words, the court was simply obeying Parliament's instruction.

In July 2015, the High Court held in *R (Davis) v Home Secretary* (2015) EWHC 2092 was incompatible with EU law, and disapplied the Act. The Court suspended the effect of the disapplication until the end of March 2016 to give Parliament the opportunity to re-legislate. Given that the court concluded that the Act breached EU law, the legal basis for suspending the disapplication of the Act is unclear.

ECA 1972 – IMPACT ON THE DOCTRINE OF IMPLIED REPEAL

Clearly, ECA 1972 has had a significant impact on the doctrine of implied repeal, under which it might have been expected that the courts would have resolved the conflict between s 2(4) ECA 1972 and the Merchant Shipping Act 1988 in favour of the later statute. In *Factortame* (1991), however, the House of Lords chose to apply the rule of construction in s 2(4) ECA 1972, setting aside the later Act.

In a sense, this choice can be seen (and was defended by Lord Bridge) as the courts actually upholding the doctrine of Parliamentary supremacy by applying a statutory rule in preference to a common law rule. This raises the question of whether Parliament itself can change the rules of its own sovereignty. Recent, post-*Factortame* case law seems to suggest that the courts would allow Parliament to do so – see the analysis of *R (Jackson) v Attorney General* (2005) (which you read about in **Chapter 5**) later in this chapter.

For the time being, it is clear from the judgments in *Factortame* (1991) and in *Thoburn* (2002) (see below) that ECA 1972 cannot be impliedly repealed, and the doctrine has to that extent been eroded.

KEY CASE: *Thoburn v Sunderland City Council* [2002] EWHC 195

Background:

T was convicted for selling bananas using non-metric measures (i.e. pounds and ounces rather than grams). An EU regulation, transposed into UK law by Regulations made under **s 2(2) ECA 1972** forbade this.

T appealed against conviction, arguing that the Weights and Measures Act 1985 permitted the sale of produce in non-metric measures, that to this extent the 1985 Act had impliedly repealed s 2(2) ECA 1972 and that the Regulations made under s 2(2) were therefore invalid.

Principle:

The High Court rejected the appeal, **LJ Laws** holding that ECA 1972 was a constitutional statute which could not be impliedly repealed:

> We should recognise a hierarchy of Acts of Parliament: as it were, 'ordinary' statutes and 'constitutional' statutes... Ordinary statutes may be impliedly repealed. Constitutional statutes may not.

We will return to the *Thoburn* case and to LJ Laws' definition of 'constitutional statute' later on in this chapter.

In *R (HS2 Action Alliance Ltd) v Secretary of State for Transport* (2014) UKSC3, the Supreme Court has developed the doctrine further, holding that constitutional statutes (in this case, the rule in Article 9 of the Bill of Rights 1689 that the courts cannot inquire into proceedings in Parliament) cannot themselves be impliedly repealed by s 2(4) ECA 1972's incorporation of EU law. This is, in a sense, the flip-side of the reasoning in *Thoburn* (2002). Lords Neuberger and Mance said:

> It is, putting the point at its lowest, certainly arguable (and it is for the United Kingdom law and courts to decide) that there may be fundamental principles, whether contained in other constitutional instruments or recognised at common law, of which Parliament when it enacted the European Communities Act 1972 did not either contemplate or authorise the abrogation.

POSSIBILITY OF EXPRESS REPEAL OF ECA 1972

When discussing the impact of EU membership on Parliamentary sovereignty, it is important to make the distinction between implied and express repeal. The UK courts have consistently made it clear that if Parliament chose to repeal ECA 1972 expressly, then they would cease to give effect to EU law. In *Macarthys Ltd v Smith* (1979) 3 All ER 32, CA, Lord Denning said:

> If the time should come when Parliament deliberately passes an Act with the intention of repudiating the Treaty or any provision in it… **and says so in express terms**… it would be the duty of our courts to follow the statute of our Parliament.

Lord Denning went on to say that he did not 'envisage any such situation'. Recent political developments in both the UK and the EU have, however, increased the possibility that the UK Parliament might choose to pass an Act which deliberately and expressly contradicts EU law, or to repeal ECA 1972 and leave the EU altogether. Parliament itself has articulated this possibility in **s 18 of the European Union Act 2011**, which provides that EU law fails is recognised in the UK only through the medium of **s 2(1) ECA 1972**. This implies that s 2(1) ECA 1972 could be expressly repealed so that EU law would no longer apply in the UK.

The UK Government has promised to hold a referendum in June 2016 on whether the UK should continue to be a member of the EU. If a majority of those voting in the referendum vote to leave the EU, then this can be achieved by Parliament repealing ECA 1972, in which case the UK courts would no longer have any basis on which to apply EU law.

INCORPORATION OF THE EUROPEAN CONVENTION ON HUMAN RIGHTS

The **Human Rights Act 1998 (HRA)** is generally considered to have adopted a relatively 'weak' method of incorporation of the Convention into UK law compared to the method by which ECA 1972 incorporated EU law. The evidence for this can be found in a comparison of the respective Acts' key provisions:

European Communities Act 1972	Human Rights Act 1998
Section 2(4) requires all UK legislation to 'be construed and have effect' subject to directly effective EU law.	**Section 3** obliges the courts to interpret Acts of Parliament in line with the Convention only 'so far as it is possible to do so'.
In *Factortame* (1991), the court took this to require it to set aside an Act of Parliament which was incompatible with EU law.	**Section 4** empowers the courts to declare a provision in an Act of Parliament incompatible with the Convention, but expressly states that such a declaration 'does not affect the validity, continuing operation or enforcement' of the provision.

(Continued)

European Communities Act 1972	Human Rights Act 1998
Section 3(1) requires UK courts to apply EU law in accordance with principles laid down by the Court of Justice of the European Union (CJEU), i.e. it makes CJEU decisions binding on UK courts.	**Section 2** requires the court to 'take into account' decisions of the European Court of Human Rights, but does not make those decisions binding on UK courts.

HRA 1998 was deliberately drafted in this way to preserve UK Parliamentary sovereignty, particularly in its express reservation of Parliament's right to legislate contrary to the Convention. Nevertheless, **ss 3 and 4 HRA 1998** have had a significant impact on the relationship between Parliament and the courts.

SECTION 3 HRA 1998 – INTERPRETATIVE OBLIGATION

There is some tension between senior judges as to how far **s 3 HRA 1998** permits the courts to 'read in' words to statutory provisions in order to interpret them in a way which is compatible with the Convention:

KEY CASE: *R v A* [2001] 3 All ER 1

Background:

Section 41(3)(c) of the Youth Justice and Criminal Evidence Act 1999 limited the circumstances in which a defendant could cross-examine a rape complainant about a previous sexual relationship.

Principle:

The House of Lords, in effect, relied on **s 3 HRA 1998** to 'read in' to that provision the words 'subject to a fair trial', so as to construe s 41 compatibly with Article 6 of the Convention. This meant interpreting it so as to allow the cross-examination of rape complainants.

Lord Steyn:

In accordance with the will of Parliament it will sometimes be necessary to adopt an interpretation which linguistically will appear strained. The techniques to be used will not only involve the reading down of express language in a statute but also the reading down of provisions. A declaration of incompatibility is a measure of last resort and must be avoided unless it is plainly impossible to do so.

Lord Hope:

[Section 3 HRA 1998 is]... only a rule of interpretation. It does not entitle the Judges to act as legislators... the compatibility is to be achieved only so far as this is possible. Plainly this will not be possible if the legislation contains provisions which expressly contradict the meaning which the enactment would have to be given to make it compatible.

The case is controversial, and split the House of Lords, with a 3:2 majority favouring Lord Steyn's interpretation. This approach has been criticised on the basis that it violates both the sovereignty of Parliament and the separation of powers. By interpreting the provision in such a way as to permit the cross-examination of rape complainants, the judges appeared to be reversing the clear intention of Parliament, as expressed in the statute. Given the sensitivities around rape proceedings, it might have been thought prior to HRA 1998 that this was an issue on which the unelected judges would defer to the will of the people's representatives in Parliament.

On the other hand, as Lord Steyn reminds us, his approach is 'in accordance with the will of Parliament', as expressed in **s 3 HRA 1998**, which requires the court to interpret statutes in line with the Convention 'where possible'. To that extent, Lord Steyn's approach conforms both to Parliamentary sovereignty and to the rule of law – both in the sense that he is applying the statutory rule of interpretation in s 3 HRA 1998 and in the sense that the rule itself appears to elevate the Convention to a code of fundamental rights to which it should be assumed, without clear and express evidence to the contrary, that Parliament intended to conform.

There are clear parallels here with the *Factortame* (1991) decision. In both cases, the decision appears to contradict the will of Parliament, but in both cases, the decisions can be explained by reference to judicial obedience to rules which Parliament itself has imposed.

SECTION 4 HRA 1998 – DECLARATIONS OF INCOMPATIBILITY

Where the courts consider themselves unable to interpret primary legislation in a way that is compatible with the Convention, they may under **s 4 HRA 1998** issue a declaration of incompatibility. Parliament deliberately stopped short of giving the courts the right to strike down an Act of Parliament on these grounds – a declaration of incompatibility does not affect the validity of the incompatible Act, which continues in force unless and until amended or repealed by Parliament.

HRA 1998 came into force in October 2000. By the end of the 2010–15 Parliament, 29 declarations of incompatibility had been issued by the courts, of which 8 had been successfully appealed by the Government (one is currently being appealed). All of the other 20 declarations have been acted on, either by the Government making a remedial order under **s 10 HRA 1998** or by Parliament enacting amending or repealing legislation to remove the incompatibility.

One of the more contentious declarations of incompatibility was made in the following case:

KEY CASE: *A v Secretary of State for the Home Department* **[2004] UKHL 56**

Background:

After the 9/11 attacks on New York, the Government derogated from (in effect, suspended) Article 5(1) of the Convention (the right to liberty) by making the Human Rights Act 1998 (Designated Derogation) Order 2001. In reliance on this derogation, Parliament enacted **s 23 of the Anti-terrorism, Crime and Security Act 2001**, which authorised the indefinite detention of foreign nationals reasonably suspected to be terrorists, unless they voluntarily left the country.

The appellants were detained under s 23 of the 2001 Act. They challenged the Derogation Order on the basis that if it was unlawful, then so was s 23 of the 2001 Act.

Principle:

The House of Lords held that:

(1)   the Government had been entitled to conclude that the conditions for a derogation were met, i.e. there was a 'public emergency' threatening the life of the nation – however, the extent of the derogation had to be 'no more than strictly necessary' to deal with the emergency;

(2)   s 23 was disproportionate because by permitting suspected terrorists to go abroad, it did not rationally address the threat they posed; and

(3)   it was also discriminatory, as it made no similar provision for detention without trial in respect of British nationals who were suspected terrorists.

Following the judgment, Parliament repealed the offending provision and replaced it with a new system of 'control orders' under s 3 of the Prevention of Terrorism Act 2005 (itself later the subject of a further declaration of incompatibility).[1]

The case is remarkable for the degree to which the court was prepared to pick apart the Government's anti-terrorist policy. Previously, the courts had been reluctant to intervene in matters of national security (see the *CCSU* (1984) case in Chapter 7). While the court deferred to the Government on its decision to declare a national emergency post-9/11, it considered that the proportionality (and therefore the legality) of the legislative response to that emergency was suitable for review by the courts. Lord Bingham, giving the leading judgment, resisted the Attorney General's argument that in doing so, the court was violating the sovereignty of Parliament and the separation of powers:

> it is the function of the courts and not of political bodies to resolve legal questions... The 1998 [Human Rights] Act gives the courts a very specific, wholly democratic mandate.

In other words, the courts have been tasked by HRA 1998 with policing the boundaries of civil liberties. This is 'wholly democratic' because the authority to do so derives from Parliament itself.

POSSIBILITY OF EXPRESS REPEAL OF HRA 1998

It is, of course, open to Parliament both to legislate expressly contrary to the Convention and to repeal HRA 1998 itself, though to do so without resigning from the Convention would leave the UK open to challenge in the European Court of Human Rights in respect of non-compatible legislation.

The UK Government has said that:

> We will scrap Labour's Human Rights Act and introduce a British Bill of Rights which will restore common sense to the application of human rights in the UK. The Bill will remain faithful to the basic principles of human rights which we signed up to in the original European Convention on Human Rights. It will protect basic rights, like the right to a fair trial, and the right to life, which are an essential part of a modern democratic society. But it will reverse the mission creep that has meant human rights law being used for more and more purposes, and often with

---

[1] *Secretary of State for Home department v JJ* [2007] UKHL 45.

little regard for the rights of wider society. Among other things the Bill will stop terrorists and other serious foreign criminals who pose a threat to our society from using spurious human rights arguments to prevent deportation.

Consultation on the content of a proposed British Bill of Rights is due to start in 2016. This is an important issue which you will need to keep up with via the news. At the time of writing, there are several important and as yet unanswered questions about what will happen if HRA 1998 is repealed. They include:

Will the UK withdraw from the European Convention on Human Rights?

Unless the UK does so, then it would seem that UK citizens will retain the right to bring a claim to the European Court of Human Rights in Strasbourg that the UK has acted incompatibly with their Convention rights. This would be more expensive and time-consuming than being able to bring such a claim in domestic courts and amounts to a return to the pre-HRA 1998 position.

Will the UK withdraw from the EU?

You have read above that there is to be a referendum on whether the UK is to stay in the EU. If a majority voted to remain in the EU, the repeal of HRA 1998 could present difficulties (depending on the content of any British Bill of Rights that replaces it) for the UK's continuing membership of the EU. For example, the European Commission has said that in negotiations for the accession of EU members, consideration is given as to whether the applicant State has shown respect for the Convention and the case law of the Strasbourg Court, and that any decision by an EU Member State to withdraw from the Convention would need to be examined under the Treaty on European Union, Article 6(3) of which states that the rights guaranteed by the Convention are general principles of EU law.

Further, the EU Charter of Fundamental Rights replicates, and in some cases goes beyond, the rights guaranteed by the Convention. The issue of prisoner voting rights, which you read about in the context of the Strasbourg Court's judgment in *Hirst* (2005) in Chapter 5, seems to have been influential in the development of the UK Government's policy of repealing HRA 1998. But in *Delvigne* (2015), the CJEU held that a French ban on prisoners voting where they had been convicted to 5 years' or more imprisonment engaged the EU Charter of Fundamental Rights, albeit that the ban was lawful in that particular case. This case raises the possibility that the UK's blanket ban on prisoner voting may be challenged as incompatible with EU law – if so, then repeal of HRA 1998 would not (unless the UK also withdraws from the EU) save the ban from being unlawful.

What will happen to human rights in Scotland and Wales?

The UK Government's policy of repealing HRA 1998 is not shared by the Governments of Scotland and Wales. Since compliance with the Convention rights incorporated by HRA 1998 is hard-wired into both the Scotland Act 1998 and the Government of Wales Act 2006 (both of which require the respective devolved legislatures and executives to act compatibly with the Convention), then repeal of HRA 1998 may, to the extent that it involves re-drawing the devolution settlements, require (not by law, but by a political convention known as the Sewel Convention) the consent of the Scottish Parliament and National Assembly for Wales.

If the UK Parliament were to legislate to alter the devolution settlements without the consent of the devolved legislatures, this could have important implications for the future of the Union – for example, it could, in Scotland, prompt calls for a further referendum on independence.

How might the judges react to the repeal of HRA 1998?

There have been a number of statements made by leading judges (whether in the context of *obiter* statements in judgments, or in speeches such as the one by Supreme Court Vice-President Lady Hale cited in the **Further reading** at the end of this chapter) which suggest that if HRA 1998 were to be repealed, the courts may apply and develop the common law to protect many of the rights which HRA 1998 currently protects.

The basis for doing so is set out by Lord Mance in *Kennedy v Charity Commission* (2014) UKSC 20:

> Since the passing of the Human Rights Act 1998 there has too often been a tendency to see the law in areas touched on by the Convention solely in terms of the Convention rights… In some areas the common law may go further than the Convention, and some contexts it may also be inspired by the Convention rights and jurisprudence… But the natural starting point in any dispute is to start with domestic law, and it is certainly not to focus exclusively on the Convention rights without surveying the wider common law scene.

So, while HRA 1998 may be repealed, the principles of the Convention rights and jurisprudence which it imported to English and Welsh law may be harder to erase.

These are difficult questions, which demonstrate the unique and complex balance between the different elements of the UK's uncodified constitution. If the politicians are able to achieve sufficient consensus on these issues for there to be a British Bill of Rights or a more fundamental codification of the constitution, how could such a Bill or document be protected against further change?

COULD PARLIAMENT ENTRENCH A CONSTITUTIONAL STATUTE?

The *Thoburn* (2002) case (see above) is notable for LJ Laws' use of the term 'constitutional statute', which he defined as follows:

Key Definition

Constitutional statute: 'In my opinion a constitutional statute is one which (a) conditions the legal relationship between citizen and state in some general, overarching manner, or (b) enlarges or diminishes the scope of what we would now regard as fundamental constitutional rights.'

LJ Laws, *Thoburn v Sunderland City Council* [2002] EWHC 195

LJ Laws went on to cite ECA 1972, HRA 1998, the Scotland Act 1998 and others as examples of what he considered to be constitutional statutes. However, this apparent judicial elevation of these Acts of Parliament to a higher (i.e. super-ordinary) status does not reflect any special measures either in the Acts themselves or in the procedure by which they were enacted. Parliament could, ultimately, repeal them by a simple majority vote, just as it could repeal an 'ordinary' Act such as the Concessionary Bus Travel Act 2007.

This begs an important question – if the judges consider these particular statutes to be superior to ordinary Acts of Parliament, would they allow Parliament to protect them by upholding statutory provisions entrenching them against amendment or repeal?

The question is particularly relevant to the UK Government's proposal to replace HRA 1998 with a British Bill of Rights. Could such a Bill be entrenched by an in-built statutory requirement to achieve a special Parliamentary majority (similar to the two-thirds majority required to change the USA's Constitution – see Chapter 2), or by a requirement to secure popular approval in a referendum, in order to change or repeal it? The question is also relevant to a proposal to amend s 1 of the Scotland Act 1998 to provide for the permanence of the Scottish Parliament.

Dicey's rules of Parliamentary sovereignty are arguably self-contradictory on this point. On the one hand, if Parliament's legislative competence is unlimited, then this should enable it to enact entrenchment provisions. On the other hand, to do so would restrict future Parliaments by making it more difficult for them to change or repeal the entrenched Act.

Since the doctrine of Parliamentary sovereignty is merely descriptive of the relationship between Parliament and the courts, we must look to evidence from the judges themselves in order to predict whether they would allow Parliament to restrict itself in this way.

There are several examples of the Privy Council (in effect, UK Supreme Court judges) accepting that Commonwealth legislatures have imposed self-limiting procedural restrictions on the manner and form in which they can enact future legislation, e.g. *Attorney General for New South Wales v Trethowan* (1932). Until recently, the status of such cases in the UK was unclear, as they involved legislatures which (unlike the UK Parliament) were established by and therefore subordinate to a codified constitution.

In the *Jackson* (2005) case (see Chapter 5), however, senior judges in the House of Lords cited these cases with approval. They accepted the legal proposition that the UK Parliament had 'redefined' the procedure by which it made legislation in the **Parliament Act 1911** by removing the requirement for the House of Lords' consent. Lord Steyn went further:

> Parliament could for specific purposes provide for a two-thirds majority in the House of Commons and the House of Lords. This would involve a redefinition of Parliament for a specific purpose. Such redefinition could not be disregarded.

Baroness Hale agreed with this proposition, saying that:

> it may very well be that Parliament could redefine itself... requiring a particular Parliamentary majority... or a popular referendum.

It is interesting that both Lord Steyn and Baroness Hale chose to air their views in support of entrenchment, given that the issue was not directly relevant to the *Jackson* (2005) case. While their comments are *obiter* and therefore not binding on future courts, they do indicate a growing mood of constitutional assertiveness among the senior judiciary.

On-the-spot question

 Section 1 of the Northern Ireland Act 1998 provides that Northern Ireland will not cease to be part of the UK without the consent of the majority of the people of Northern Ireland voting in a poll.

If a future UK Parliament legislated for Northern Ireland to break free from the UK without such consent, how would the courts treat this provision?

SUMMARY

- Parliamentary sovereignty is a common law rule, which (in the absence of a codified constitution) describes the relationship between Parliament and the courts. Under the rule, the courts recognise and give effect to Acts of Parliament as the highest form of law.
- Because it is a common law rule, Parliamentary sovereignty is flexible and can be altered both by statute and by the courts themselves. ECA 1972, while it remains in force, has altered the rule by requiring the courts to give effect to Acts of Parliament only to the extent that they do not contradict EU law: see *Factortame* (1991).
- While the Human Rights Act 1998 expressly preserves the right of Parliament to legislate contrary to the Convention and does not allow the courts to strike down an incompatible Act, it has increased the courts' powers of review and influence over Parliamentary legislation: see *R v A* (2001) and *A v Secretary of State for the Home Department* (2004). As a result, there appears to have been a change in judicial culture, from one of unquestioning acceptance of Acts of Parliament to one of active judicial scrutiny:

  > Judges nowadays have no alternative but to apply the Human Rights Act 1998. Constitutional dangers exist no less in too little judicial activism as in too much. There are limits to the legitimacy of executive or legislative decision-making, just as there are to decision-making by the courts.
  > Simon Brown LJ, *International Transport Roth GmbH v Secretary of State for the Home Department* [2003] QB 728

- Further evidence of 'judicial activism' can be seen in the courts' prioritisation of 'constitutional statutes' in *Thoburn* (2002) and their apparent willingness in *Jackson* (2005) to allow Parliament to entrench such statutes against amendment or repeal. It can also be seen in the suggestion in *AXA* (2011) that Acts of Parliament may be subject to review against the fundamental principles of the rule of law, and in the assertion of the common law as a source of protection for fundamental rights, possibly in anticipation of repeal of HRA 1998.

FURTHER READING

Craig, P, 'Constitutionalising constitutional law: HS2' [2014] *Public Law* 373–92 – analyses the Supreme Court's approach to the relationship between Parliamentary sovereignty, EU law, and fundamental instruments and principles of UK constitutional law.

Goldsworthy, J, *Parliamentary Sovereignty: Contemporary Debates*, 2010, Cambridge: Cambridge University Press – a detailed examination of the legal basis for Parliamentary sovereignty, and the impact upon the doctrine of key legislation and cases, including *Factortame* and *Thoburn*.

Lady Hale, 'UK constitutionalism on the march' (12 July 2014), available at www.supremecourt. uk/docs/speech-140712.pdf – a speech by Supreme Court Vice-President Lady Hale to the Constitutional and Administrative Law Bar Association Conference 2014, in which she discusses the resurgence of common law fundamental rights, and the relationship between EU law and other fundamental constitutional principles. Essential reading and a great source of further case law.

Ronchi, P, 'AXA v Lord Advocate: putting the AXA to Parliamentary sovereignty' (2013) *European Public Law* 19(1), 61–71 – discusses the significance of the Supreme Court's decision and the *obiter* suggestion that the Court may consider there to be limits on Parliament's ability to legislate to curtain fundamental rights.

Sales, P, 'Judges and legislature: values into law' (2012) *Cambridge Law Journal* 71(2), 287–96 – considers the impact of ECA 1972 and HRA 1998 on judicial statutory interpretation.

Wagner, Adam, 'Does Parliamentary sovereignty still reign supreme?', available at www.guardian. co.uk/law/2011/jan/27/supreme-court-parliamentary-sovereignty – an article by Adam Wagner, barrister and editor of the UK Human Rights Blog, on the complex relationship between Parliament, the Supreme Court and the European Convention on Human Rights.

www.parliament.uk/business/committees/committees-a-z/lords-select/eu-justice-subcommittee/ inquiries/parliament-2015/potential-impact-of-repealing-the-human-rights-act-on-eu-law – the Parliamentary EU Justice Sub-Committee's home page for its inquiry into the impact of repealing HRA 1998 on EU law. You can access the views of a variety of expert witnesses.

COMPANION WEBSITE

An online glossary compiled by the author is available on the companion website: www.routledge.com/cw/beginningthelaw

Chapter 7

Government's relationship with Parliament

LEARNING OBJECTIVES

After reading this chapter, you should be able to:

- Explain the composition and structure of Government
- Discuss prerogative powers and the adequacy of controls upon them
- Understand the importance of conventions in regulating Government
- Evaluate Parliamentary scrutiny of Government.

INTRODUCTION

In Chapter 5 we traced the development of Parliamentary sovereignty as the central principle of the UK's uncodified constitution, while noting that in reality Parliament tends to be dominated by the political party (or coalition of parties) that happens to be in Government at any particular time. This chapter considers Government in detail.

We will begin by examining the personnel and structure of Government, and will then discuss the constitutional relationship between Government and Parliament; in particular, the effectiveness of uncodified conventions in holding Government to account and recent proposals to transfer important Government prerogative powers to Parliament.

THE QUEEN'S ROLE IN GOVERNMENT

The reigning monarch (currently Queen Elizabeth II) is the Head of State, i.e. the ceremonial Head of Government, which is carried on by Ministers (headed by the Prime Minister) as agents on Her Majesty's behalf.

In terms of the Queen's influence upon those Ministers, Walter Bagehot described the role of the monarch as 'to advise, encourage and to warn'. As Rodney Brazier has pointed out,[1]

---

[1] Rodney Brazier, 'The Monarchy' in V Bogdanor (ed), *The British Constitution in the Twentieth Century* (2003, Oxford: British Academy/Oxford University Press), Chapter 3, p 78.

this requires that the Queen is also kept informed and in some cases consulted about Government action. According to the official website of the British Monarchy:

> Although she is a constitutional monarch who remains politically neutral… the Queen gives a weekly audience to the Prime Minister at which she has a right and a duty to express her views on Government matters… These meetings remain strictly confidential. Having expressed her views, the Queen abides by the advice of her Ministers.[2]

We saw in Chapters 2, 3 and 5 that the Queen exercises constitutionally significant legal powers, but that they are in practice exercised in accordance with political conventions. These **prerogative powers** (see below) include the following powers in relation to Government appointments:

Legal power exercisable by the monarch	Convention
Power to appoint the Prime Minister.	The Queen appoints the person who can command the confidence of the House of Commons, e.g. the leader of the party with an overall majority of Commons seats.
Power to appoint and dismiss other Government Ministers at Her Majesty's pleasure.	The Queen appoints and dismisses Ministers on the advice, and at the request, of the Prime Minister.

These conventions are neither codified nor legally binding. Further **prerogative powers** exercised by Government Ministers on behalf of the Queen are discussed below.

THE STRUCTURE OF GOVERNMENT

The Prime Minister

The role of Prime Minister, the most important political office in the UK, is almost entirely uncodified and has evolved by convention.

While there is little specific statutory power afforded to the office, in reality the Prime Minister leads and controls discussion in **the Cabinet** (see below), whose members he, in effect, selects (see the conventions relating to the exercise of legal powers by **the Crown**

[2] www.royal.gov.uk/MonarchUK/QueenandGovernment/QueenandPrimeMinister.aspx, accessed 9 January 2016.

above). He is responsible for the overall organisation and leadership of the Government, and for allocating functions to Ministers and their departments, which he may, at his discretion, re-structure. The Prime Minister also exercises the **prerogative power** (see below) to declare war and to deploy the armed forces, and represents the Government in European Council meetings, which determine the general political direction and priorities of the EU.

Given the extensive power wielded by the Prime Minister, it is perhaps surprising (particularly to non-UK students) that the electorate do not get to vote directly for who should hold the office. By convention, it is expected that the Prime Minister is an elected MP who can command the support of a majority of MPs in the House of Commons.

Should the Prime Minister, having been appointed by the Queen according to this convention, resign or die between General Elections, there is no requirement for a further election to be held. In effect, the party (or parties) in Government nominate a new leader, whom they ask the Queen to appoint – e.g. Gordon Brown took over as Labour Party leader and was subsequently appointed Prime Minister following the resignation of Tony Blair in 2007.

This means that while the Prime Minister is 'first among equals' in the **Cabinet**, he is ultimately dependent on the continuing support of his Cabinet colleagues and his party in order to remain in office. For example, the events which ultimately brought about the resignation from office of Margaret Thatcher, the longest-serving Prime Minister since World War II, were catalysed by the resignation from the Cabinet of Geoffrey Howe MP, following which he made a speech in Parliament criticising the Prime Minister's stance on the proposal for the UK to adopt the euro (a common European currency) and her style of leadership:

> It is rather like sending your opening batsmen to the crease only for them to find … that their bats have been broken before the game by the team captain.[3]

On-the-spot question

? What if, at the next General Election, no single party secured an overall majority of seats in the House of Commons? If the parties are unable to agree on who should form a coalition Government, who should the Queen appoint as Prime Minister? How would the Queen decide?

---

[3] 'Sir Geoffrey Howe savages Prime Minister over European stance in resignation speech', *The Times*, 14 November 1990.

The Cabinet

The Cabinet is a committee of senior Government Ministers, headed (and, in effect, selected) by the Prime Minister. The Cabinet collectively takes the major strategic and operational decisions which set the agenda for Government – in much the same way as a board of directors runs a company. Most Cabinet Ministers head a particular Government Department and have the title 'Secretary of State', e.g. the Foreign Secretary heads the Foreign Office. The role of the Cabinet is to formulate Government policy, i.e. to agree in principle the legislative proposals which the Government is to introduce into Parliament and to determine how the Government should use its existing legal powers.

During the 1980s and 1990s, the importance of the Cabinet in the Government decision-making process declined – for example, the decision to transfer control of interest rates to the Bank of England in 1997 was taken by Tony Blair (then Prime Minister) and Gordon Brown (then Chancellor of the Exchequer) without consulting the Cabinet.

This usage of a so-called 'kitchen Cabinet', i.e. a sub-group of the Prime Minister's most valued and trusted Cabinet Members (and in some cases, unelected personal special advisers – see below) to take decisions which the Cabinet is then expected to 'rubber-stamp' has been criticised, in particular by the Butler Review into the intelligence which led the UK to go to war in Iraq in 2003:

> we are concerned that the informality and circumscribed character of the Government's procedures which we saw in the context of policy-making towards Iraq risks reducing the scope for informed collective political judgment.
>
> Butler Committee, *Review of Intelligence on Weapons of Mass Destruction*, 2004

Non-Cabinet Ministers

Below Cabinet level, there are further Ministers and Parliamentary Under-Secretaries of State who assist the relevant Cabinet Ministers to manage the work of their respective Departments, e.g. by taking responsibility for a particular policy area, such as the Minister of Immigration, who currently serves under the Home Secretary (the Cabinet member responsible for the Home Office). The **House of Commons Disqualification Act 1975** limits the number of paid Ministers in the House of Commons to 95.

Attorney General

The Attorney General is a Minister who attends Cabinet, is the chief legal adviser to the Government and represents the Government in court proceedings. The Attorney General also has certain roles and responsibilities in relation to criminal justice, e.g. in giving consent to the prosecution of certain offences and in supervising the work of the Crown Prosecution Service and Serious Fraud Office.

There are concerns that the political nature of the Attorney General's office (the Attorney General is appointed and holds office on the advice of the Prime Minister) is incompatible with his legal duties. Recent high-profile and controversial issues involving the Attorney General include:

- Disclosure of the Attorney General's advice on the legality of going to war in Iraq and allegations that the advice disclosed to Parliament differed from that given to the Government (2003).
- Discontinuation, on the grounds of national security, of an investigation by the Serious Fraud Office into alleged bribes by BAE Systems plc to Saudi Arabian Government officials (2007).
- The Attorney General's role in the 'cash for honours' investigation, in which it was alleged that recommendations for life peerages had been made by the Prime Minister in return for donations to his political party. The Attorney General obtained an injunction to prevent the BBC from broadcasting an item about the investigation, saying that he had acted 'completely independently of government'.[4] Ultimately, the Crown Prosecution Service decided not to bring any prosecutions in the matter (2007).

In July 2009, following extensive public consultation on the role of the Attorney General, the then Labour Government decided (contrary to the Parliamentary Justice Committee's recommendations) not to bring forward any legislation to reform the office.

The office remains controversial, however, because the fact that the Attorney General is a political appointee arguably compromises the independence and impartiality of the office – at least in appearance, if not in reality. The vulnerability of the Attorney General arguably compromises the ability of the office holder to give full, frank and fearless advice to the Government that he serves, as perhaps evidenced by the removal of Dominic Grieve MP from the post in July 2014 after he repeatedly pointed out apparent legal and political difficulties in the Conservative Government's position on repeal of the Human Rights Act 1998 and continuing membership of the European Convention on Human Rights.

Also, the Attorney General retains responsibilities in relation to advising Parliament about the rules of Parliamentary proceedings and the conduct of MPs. Given that Parliament is supposed to scrutinise the Government and hold Ministers accountable for their actions, it is difficult to reconcile the multiple roles of the Attorney General with either the doctrine of the separation of powers or the fundamental principle that lawyers must avoid conflicts of interest.

[4] Reported at http://news.bbc.co.uk/1/hi/6414113.stm, 3 March 2007.

Commenting on this in a recent article in the *Public Law* journal (see **Further reading** at the end of this chapter) calling for the abolition of the office of Attorney General and the redistribution of his functions to independent lawyers, Alec Samuels has said that:

> By convention, amounting virtually to a rule of law, in discharging his legal duties the Attorney-General acts independently and in the public interest, whatever his political views and affiliations... The genius of the English is to make old, irrational, illogical and anomalous institutions work surprisingly well, principally due to the integrity of the office holders. The office of Attorney-General is long-standing and honourable but undeniably and irredeemably anomalous.

On-the-spot question

 Is the office of Attorney General an example of the UK's uncodified constitutional arrangements working well despite, or because of, the absence of a formalised separation of powers?

Government whips

Whips co-ordinate the voting of Government MPs and advise on promotions, so they wield considerable power within the party. Whips also act as a line of communication between the Government and backbench MPs (see Chapter 5).

Government Departments and civil servants

Although a Minister is ultimately responsible (see below) for the work of each Government Department, in practice much of the day-to-day administrative work is done by politically independent civil servants. Their job is to give impartial and confidential advice to Ministers, and to assist the Government of the day in formulating and implementing its policies. Civil servants generally retain their jobs following a change of Government after a General Election – they are appointed and dismissed by other civil servants, and not by Ministers.

Special advisers

Special advisers are defined in **s 15 of the Constitutional Reform and Governance Act 2010** as civil servants appointed 'to assist a Minister of the Crown after being selected for that appointment by that Minister personally'. Their appointment must be approved by the Prime Minister. Essentially, special advisers (or 'SpAds') are temporary civil servants who each have a close relationship with a particular Minister and will normally resign should that Minister leave office.

Following concerns about the growing influence of SpAds over independent civil servants during the Blair Government (e.g. Jo Moore, a SpAd in the Department of Transport, Local Government and the Regions, infamously instructed departmental civil servants that 11 September 2001 would be 'a good day to bury bad news'), a Code of Conduct was developed to clarify the boundaries between special advisers and non-political civil servants. The Code defines the role of special advisers as follows:

> Special advisers are a critical part of the team supporting Ministers. They add a political dimension to the advice and assistance available to Ministers while reinforcing the political impartiality of the permanent Civil Service by distinguishing the source of political advice and support.[5]

THE POWERS OF GOVERNMENT

The rule of law (see Chapter 4) requires that the Government does not act without a clear legal authority to do so. Most Government powers derive from Acts of Parliament. However, there is a residue of historical common law powers, known as **prerogative powers**, formerly exercised by the monarch, but now exercised on behalf of the Crown by Ministers. These are small in number, yet are constitutionally very important.

Statutory powers

Acts of Parliament frequently set out a legal framework within which Ministers can take decisions or 'fill in the detail' needed to implement a policy by making delegated legislation. Parliament (through the enabling Act) confers and sets the limits of Governmental powers in these areas. As we will see in Chapter 8, the courts have developed the doctrine of judicial review to make sure that the Government stays within these limits.

Prerogative powers

Key Definition

Prerogative powers:

> The residue of discretionary or arbitrary authority which at any given time is legally left in the hands of the Crown.
>
> A V Dicey, *Introduction to the Study of the Law of the Constitution* (1885)

---

[5] Code of Conduct for Special Advisers, para 1 (as amended October 2015).

> In most modern democracies, the government's only powers are those granted to it by a written constitution or by the legislature. A distinguishing feature of the British constitution is the extent to which government continues to exercise a number of powers which were not granted to it by a written constitution, nor by Parliament, but are, rather, ancient prerogatives of the Crown.
>
> *The Governance of Britain*, Command Paper CM 7170, July 2007

Background

Prerogative powers are a 'hangover' from the historical concept of the 'divine right' of kingship, under which the monarch was all-powerful. Abuses of royal power led the courts to be more assertive in defending the rule of law, so that in the *Case of Proclamations* (1610) it was held that the monarch's power was restricted to those areas recognised by the courts:

The King hath no prerogative but that which the law of the land allows him.

As political power gradually transferred from the monarchy to Parliament (see Chapter 5), the scope of prerogative powers was eroded. Parliament has legislated in many areas formerly within the scope of the prerogative. Where it has done so, the common law doctrine of Parliamentary sovereignty (see Chapter 6) has led the courts to treat the Act of Parliament as having extinguished and replaced the prerogative power.

There remain, however, important policy areas in which statute has not yet encroached on prerogative powers.

Prerogative powers – examples

In the absence of a codified constitution, there is no single authoritative and exhaustive list of prerogative powers. The prerogative is a common law phenomenon and exists only to the extent recognised by the courts.

In addition to those prerogative powers exercised personally by the Queen (such as the power to appoint the Prime Minister – see above), examples of prerogative powers in domestic affairs include:

- the power to grant mercy to convicted criminals;
- the power to create or abolish a Government Department;
- the power to keep the peace within the UK;
- civil emergency powers (although this is increasingly an area on which Parliament legislates);

- the granting of honours;
- the incorporation of bodies (e.g. the British Broadcasting Corporation) by Royal Charter.

Examples of prerogative powers in the context of international affairs include:

- the power to declare war and deploy the armed forces (see below);
- the power to make treaties – though the **European Union Act 2011** requires a referendum in order to amend the Treaty on European Union (see below);
- the power to issue passports.

Parliamentary control of the prerogative

Parliament can legislate to codify, abolish or curtail prerogative powers. Where it does so, the courts will usually treat the Act of Parliament as having extinguished and replaced the former prerogative power.

For example, in *Burmah Oil v Lord Advocate* (1965) (see Chapter 6), Parliament, by enacting the War Damage Act 1965, abolished the prerogative power which required compensation to be paid to UK subjects whose property had been destroyed, replacing it with a statutory scheme.

The power of Parliament to control the prerogative via statute depends, however, on the willingness of the Government to promote and support appropriate legislation. The extent to which Parliament can influence, or even scrutinise, the use of prerogative powers also depends on political circumstances.

This is illustrated by recent developments in the relationship between Parliament and the Government over the exercise of the prerogative power to deploy the armed forces. It began with the Parliamentary debate on the Government's proposal to go to war in Iraq in 2003. Legally, the Government could have committed the armed forces to conflict in reliance on prerogative powers, without any reference to Parliament. However, in light of considerable public and Parliamentary opposition to the war, the Government invited Parliament to debate, and vote upon, the proposal.

There are two ways of looking at this – on the one hand, the fact that public and political pressure persuaded the Government to hold such a debate might be seen as a triumph for democracy; on the other hand, it might be argued that such a debate should be a constitutional pre-requisite for such an important decision and should not depend on what William Hague MP (then in opposition) described as 'an act of generosity by the Government for which we had to be grateful at the time'.[6]

---

[6] In evidence to the Select Committee on Public Administration; see Fourth Report, Session 2003–04, 4 March 2004.

In 2011 William Hague (then Foreign Secretary) stated during a House of Commons debate on military action in Libya that 'we will… enshrine in law for the future the necessity of consulting Parliament on military action'.[7] Parliament has not yet legislated for this, but the strength of the political imperative to seek Parliamentary approval for deployment of the armed forces is demonstrated by the fact that when Parliament declined to support a Government proposal to carry out air strikes in Syria in 2013, the Government respected its decision. The Government did not exercise the prerogative power to take military action in Syria until Parliament, having been asked to reconsider the matter in December 2015 following terrorist attacks in Paris, voted to approve air strikes. In the absence of statutory controls over this prerogative power, it appears that a convention is emerging that the Government will seek Parliamentary approval prior to its exercise.

Judicial control of the prerogative

The courts have made it clear that the prerogative is residual, i.e. no new prerogative powers can be claimed:

> It is 350 years and a civil war too late for the Queen's courts to broaden the prerogative.
>
> LJ Diplock, *BBC v Johns* [1965] Ch 32

This decision, however, is hard to reconcile with the decision in *R v Secretary of State for the Home Department ex p Northumbria Police Authority* (1989) QB 26, CA, in which the Court of Appeal recognised a prerogative power to keep the peace which authorised the keeping of CS gas and baton rounds, despite the fact that no previous authority for such a power could be found.

Applying the doctrine of Parliamentary sovereignty, the courts have prevented the Government from relying on *existing* prerogative powers in order to evade statutory provisions in an Act of Parliament – even, as in *R v Secretary of State for the Home Department ex p Fire Brigades Union* (1994) 2 WLR 1, CA, where the relevant provisions of the Act of Parliament have not yet been brought into force.

The extent to which the courts are prepared to interfere with the Government's use of prerogative powers depends, however, on what the courts consider to be the 'justiciability' of the issue in question:

---

[7] Reported in *Hansard*, HC Deb, 21 March 2011, col 799.

KEY CASE: *Council of Civil Services Unions (CCSU) v Minister for the Civil Service* **[1984] 3 All ER 935**

Background:

The Prime Minister (who was also the Minister for the Civil Service) decided that, in the interests of national security, civil servants employed in intelligence work at the Government Communications Headquarters would not be allowed to be members of a trade union. This decision was enforced through an Order in Council, made in reliance on the prerogative power to administer the civil service. The affected civil servants challenged the Order by an application for judicial review (see Chapter 8).

Principle:

The House of Lords held that while prerogative powers were in principle reviewable by the courts, it was not prepared to interfere with measures taken by the Prime Minister where issues of national security were involved.

Lord Scarman:

> It is par excellence a non-justiciable question. The judicial process is totally inept to deal with the sort of problems which [national security] involves.

A distinction can therefore be made between exercises of prerogative powers which involve questions of 'high policy', such as national security or international relations, and are non-justiciable, and decisions taken under prerogative powers which are administrative in nature and limited to particular individuals or groups, as in *R v Secretary of State for Foreign and Commonwealth Affairs ex p Everett* (1989) QB 811, [1989] 1 All ER 655, CA, in which a refusal to issue a passport was upheld by the Court of Appeal.

On-the-spot question

? Do you think that statutory codification of the prerogative power to deploy the armed forces is necessary or appropriate? What practical difficulties can you foresee with drafting the necessary legislation? Would a convention requiring Parliamentary approval provide sufficient democratic control?

Reform of prerogative powers

The Labour Government promised in July 2007 to surrender or limit its prerogative powers, which it considered to be 'no longer appropriate in a modern democracy' (*The Governance* of Britain).[8] Its *Review of Executive Royal Prerogative Powers*, published in October 2009, is the first time that a Government has attempted to produce a consolidated list of prerogative powers. The list is not legally binding, but may be influential in future disputes about the existence or scope of prerogative powers.

The **Constitutional Renewal and Governance Act 2010**, however, delivered only piecemeal reform to the prerogative. The Act codified some (but not all) of the Government's powers to manage the civil service and gave legal effect to a House of Commons resolution preventing the Government from ratifying a Treaty. The House of Lords can also pass a resolution against ratification, to which the Government must respond, but which does not prevent ratification. The Act contained no measures about prerogative powers to declare war or about the issue of passports.

Following the 2010 General Election, piecemeal reform of the prerogative continued. Parliament enacted the **European Union Act 2011**, which provides that a Treaty amending either the **Treaty on European Union** or the **Treaty on the Functioning of the European Union** is invalid unless it has been approved by (a) an Act of Parliament and (b) the UK's electorate in a referendum. The **Fixed-term Parliaments Act 2011** has also codified the law in relation to the timing of General Elections (see Chapter 5), which were previously subject to the prerogative power to dissolve Parliament, exercised by convention at the Prime Minister's request.

When answering questions on reform of prerogative powers or constitutional reform more generally, it is useful to be able to refer to these examples. A critical discussion of them might consider whether this piecemeal approach to reform is motivated by political expediency (e.g. whether the **Fixed-term Parliaments Act 2011** was designed to prolong the life of what was then a coalition Government) rather than by any grand and coherent constitutional design.

CONVENTIONS AND MINISTERIAL RESPONSIBILITY

We have considered above the role played by conventions in appointing the Prime Minister and the Cabinet. Conventions also regulate the relationship between the Government and Parliament. In particular, there are two important, but arguably contradictory, conventions relating to Ministerial responsibility.

---

[8] www.peerage.org/genealogy/royal-prerogative.pdf.

Individual Ministerial responsibility

In Chapter 3 we examined the convention that Ministers are answerable to Parliament for the conduct of both their Department and the officials who work in it. We found that the doctrine has evolved from one of 'responsibility' (i.e. Ministers being expected to take the blame for Departmental errors, as in the Crichel Down affair) into one of 'accountability' (i.e. Ministers being expected merely to explain or 'account for' such errors).

Parliamentary Select Committees (which you read about in Chapter 5) play an important role in scrutinising Government Departments and holding to account the Ministers who are responsible for them. This plays a vital role in 'keeping Ministers honest', which is important to the maintenance of public confidence in Government, Parliament and the democratic process as a whole.

A major political scandal in 2009 about MPs abusing the Parliamentary expenses system had significantly undermined public trust in Parliament, particularly since the wrongdoing of MPs had been exposed primarily by the media rather than by internal checks and scrutiny processes in Parliament itself. This led to the creation of the Independent Parliamentary Standards Authority to oversee and regulate MPs' business costs and expenses instead of leaving this to Parliamentary self-regulation.

Collective Ministerial responsibility

Essentially, this requires Cabinet (and other) Ministers to present a united front. While Ministers may in private discussions (i.e. at Cabinet meetings) disagree with and criticise Government policy, they are required to support and defend that policy in Parliament and in public. This in turn requires that details of Cabinet meetings are kept confidential.

KEY CASE: *Attorney General v Jonathan Cape Ltd* [1975] 3 WLR 606

Background:

The Attorney General applied to court for an injunction to prevent Jonathan Cape Ltd from publishing the diaries of the former Cabinet Minister Richard Crossman, on the grounds that the diaries contained records of confidential Cabinet discussions and advice to Ministers, and that publication would therefore be damaging to the doctrine of Cabinet collective responsibility.

> Principle:
>
> The court recognised the importance of Cabinet confidentiality and the existence of
> a convention collective Ministerial responsibility, but was not prepared to grant the
> injunction requested as the convention was not legally binding.

By convention, any Minister who no longer feels able to support Government policy
in public must resign. Examples from Tony Blair's Labour Government include the
resignations of Robin Cook MP and Clare Short MP from the Cabinet in connection with the
Government's decision to go to war in Iraq in 2003.

Collective responsibility originated from a political need for Parliament and Ministers to
present a united front against the monarch. It is questionable how democratic a doctrine
it is in contemporary society. On the one hand, the convention of collective responsibility
requires the Government as a whole to resign if defeated on a 'no confidence' motion in
the Commons, but on the other hand, it hinders the accountability of individual Ministers to
Parliament, as Ministers are able to claim that decisions were taken collectively. Arguably, it
is also rather at odds with the idea of open and transparent Government.

The convention of collective responsibility is also based on the idea that the decision
ultimately reached by the Cabinet has been the subject of full, frank and uninhibited prior
discussion. As discussed above in relation to the 'kitchen Cabinet' of the Blair Government,
and the Butler Committee's criticisms of policy-making prior to the 2003 Iraq war, this has
not always been the case where a General Election results in a single party holding a large
controlling majority in the House of Commons. The party's success is usually attributed to
its leader, who then as Prime Minister exerts a correspondingly powerful influence over
Ministerial colleagues in Cabinet.

SUMMARY

- The Government consists of the Prime Minister and other Ministers appointed
  by the Queen. By convention, the Prime Minister is the leader of the party (or
  coalition of parties) which has a majority of MPs in the House of Commons.
- Non-legal conventions play an important role in regulating the relationships
  between the Queen, Government Ministers and Parliament.
- While many of the Government's powers are statutory, and to that extent are
  democratically defined by Parliament, there remain some important common
  law prerogative powers (such as the power to commit the UK armed forces to
  military action) which are uncodified, ill-defined and arguably are not subject to
  full Parliamentary or judicial control.

FURTHER READING

Phillipson, G, '"Historic" Commons' Syria vote: the constitutional significance (Parts I and II)', UK Constitutional Law Blog (19 September 2013), available at http://ukconstitutionallaw.org – this analyses the developing relationship between Parliament and the Government over the exercise of the prerogative power to take military action.

Samuels, A, 'Abolish the office of Attorney General' [2014] *Public* Law 609–14 – this points out inconsistencies between the multiple roles of the Attorney General and the doctrine of the separation of powers, and calls for reform.

Wright, A, *British Politics: A Very Short Introduction*, 2003, Oxford: Oxford Paperbacks – an accessible, entertaining, insider's view of the relationship between the Government, Parliament and the electorate from a former Labour MP and Chairman of the House of Commons Public Administration Select Committee.

www.gov.uk/government/how-government-works – this contains useful information about the structure of Cabinet Government, and both the identities and responsibilities of current Government Departments and Ministers.

www.gov.uk/government/speeches/parliament-and-the-judiciary – a speech by then Attorney General, Dominic Grieve MP on 25 October 2012 setting out the incumbent holder's view of the role and responsibilities of the office.

http://researchbriefings.files.parliament.uk/documents/SN03861/SN03861.pdf – House of Commons Research Briefing on Government prerogative powers and proposals for their reform.

www.telegraph.co.uk/news/newstopics/mps-expenses – the *Daily Telegraph* newspaper broke the story and led the media investigation into the Parliamentary expenses scandal of 2009. The newspaper's landing page for that topic details the investigation and contains links to more recent controversies about MPs' behaviour.

COMPANION WEBSITE

An online glossary compiled by the author is available on the companion website: www.routledge.com/cw/beginningthelaw

Chapter 8
Government and the courts

LEARNING OBJECTIVES

After reading this chapter, you should be able to:

- Explain how judges are appointed
- Understand the importance of Government being subject to legal controls
- Discuss the role of judicial review within the UK's uncodified constitution
- Understand the basic principle of judicial review, and apply them to a factual problem.

INTRODUCTION

In Chapter 7 we considered Government's relationship with Parliament. In theory, Government is subject to Parliamentary control, both in terms of the legal limits imposed on Government by Acts of Parliament and the scrutiny of Government spending and action by MPs. In reality, however, the UK has a weak separation of powers and a Government with a strong, loyal majority has a dominant influence in the House of Commons, able to control the timing of debates and to pass legislation at will. This can undermine the effectiveness of Parliamentary scrutiny and control.

The separation of powers between Government and the judiciary is, however, much greater. Given the potential for the UK's first past the post voting system to return an 'elective dictatorship', judicial independence and assertiveness is vital in ensuring that Government is subject to the rule of law. In this chapter, we will first consider how judges are appointed. We will then explore, in outline, the principles of judicial review – a key administrative law mechanism enabling citizens to seek redress against the Government and other public bodies that have acted illegally, unreasonably, disproportionately or unfairly.

HOW ARE JUDGES APPOINTED?

Judges used to be appointed by the Lord Chancellor, whose office (until the **Constitutional Reform Act 2005**) combined the roles of Cabinet Minister, Presiding Officer of the House of Lords and head of the judiciary. This combination of roles clearly violated the doctrine of separation of powers – uniquely, the Lord Chancellor was involved in all three branches of State.

The Constitutional Reform Act 2005 transferred the Lord Chancellor's legislative functions to the Speaker of the House of Lords, his executive functions to the Secretary of State for Constitutional Affairs (now, following departmental re-organisation, the Secretary of State for Justice) and his judicial functions to the Lord Chief Justice (see below). The Act also removed the judicial function from the House of Lords, creating a new Supreme Court physically and legally separate from Parliament. The office of Lord Chancellor is now combined with that of Secretary of State for Justice – the most recent incumbents have been members of the House of Commons, as well as serving Cabinet Ministers.

While the Ministry of Justice is responsible for resourcing and funding the Courts Service, the Government is no longer responsible for judicial appointments. Instead, judges are now selected by the **Judicial Appointments Commission**, an independent body comprising members of the judiciary, the legal profession, magistrates and members of the public. The Commission has a statutory duty under the 2005 Act to:

- select candidates only on merit;
- select only people of good character;
- have regard to the need to encourage diversity in the range of persons available for judicial selection.

For further details on the Commission's selection process and its relationship with the Ministry of Justice (which sponsors the Commission), visit http://jac.judiciary.gov.uk/index.htm.

The Commission convenes a special panel to appoint the Lord Chief Justice, who is Head of Criminal Justice and President of the Courts of England and Wales, and the most senior judge in the country. He also has overall responsibility for the deployment of judges and the allocation of work to the courts, as well as representing judges' views to Parliament and Government, e.g. when being consulted about the viability of new legislation.

These arrangements provide a formal structure in which the judiciary has access to Parliament and Government, but is legally and institutionally separated from the legislature and the executive. They offer further evidence of the enormous impact of the Human Rights Act 1998 (HRA 1998) on the UK's constitution.

WHY DOES JUDICIAL INDEPENDENCE MATTER?

The Judicial Appointments Commission is ultimately funded by the taxpayer. Prior to enactment of the Constitutional Reform Act 2005, many politicians, judges and members of the legal profession questioned whether the expense of reforming the Lord Chancellor's office was necessary or desirable, pointing out that there had been few serious challenges to the independence of the judiciary under the old arrangements and adopting an 'if it ain't broke, don't fix it' attitude. Others felt that it was important not only that judges *were* independent, but that they were *seen* to be independent, and that this required a transparent selection process.

The impetus to unpick the Lord Chancellor's multiple roles, after several centuries of clear non-compliance with the doctrine of the separation of powers, came from HRA 1998, which incorporated the European Convention on Human Rights (the Convention) into UK law. The Lord Chancellor's position was clearly incompatible with **Article 6 of the Convention**, which requires an independent and impartial judge or tribunal in order to guarantee a fair trial. In *McGonnell v UK* (2000) 30 EHRR 289, the European Court of Human Rights had held that the overlapping judicial, executive and legislative roles of the Bailiff of Guernsey breached Article 6, necessitating reform.

Sections 3 and 4 HRA 1998 direct the judges to review Acts of Parliament for their compatibility with the Convention, interpreting them to give effect to Convention rights where possible, and otherwise issuing a declaration of incompatibility (you read about this in Chapter 6). As you will see later in this chapter and in Chapter 9, HRA 1998 also gives judges the responsibility for reviewing the compatibility of executive action with the Convention, directing the courts to strike down secondary legislation and to declare other incompatible executive actions (and failures to act) unlawful.

As we saw in Chapter 6 when we examined the judgments in *R v A* (2001), and *A v Secretary of State for the Home Department* (2004), HRA 1998 requires the judges, on occasions, to make politically contentious decisions. In order for judges to perform their role with credibility and public confidence, it is therefore vital that they are seen to be independent of both Parliament and the Government.

More broadly, the rule of law (see Chapter 2) requires that the Government and other public bodies should be subject to legal limits, and cannot operate above the law. So where Parliament confers powers on a public body, the courts supervise the exercise of those powers and ensure that the public body does not exceed any limits imposed by the enabling Act.

The rule of law also requires that public bodies should deal with citizens fairly and behave in a way which conforms to judicially recognised standards of 'natural justice'. The courts have developed these standards through a succession of cases in which they have held that certain public bodies have acted unfairly, e.g. by making a biased decision or by not giving adequate reasons for their decision.

This body of case law is known as administrative law. The process by which cases are brought before the courts is known as judicial review.

THE CONSTITUTIONAL ROLE OF JUDICIAL REVIEW

Under the traditional doctrine of the separation of powers, Parliament makes laws, the Government (and other public bodies) run the country according to those laws and the courts adjudicate on disputes as to whether or not the Government is acting within those laws.

There are differences of opinion as to the extent to which judicial review conforms to the separation of powers. These can best be summarised through the 'traffic light' theory of the constitution we examined in Chapter 4:

Group	Constitutional perspective	Attitude to judicial review
'Red light'	Government should be tightly controlled, as it threatens civil liberties.	Judicial review is a vital legal safeguard against Government exceeding or abusing its powers.
'Amber light'	Freedom to govern should be balanced with respect for the law, and for basic principles of reasonableness and fairness.	Judicial review should provide a limited right of challenge to public bodies, where the public interest requires it.
'Green light'	Government should be free to use its powers to act in citizens' best interests.	As the scope and intensity of judicial review increases, there is a danger that unelected judges will take decisions best left to elected politicians.

Judicial review and Parliamentary supremacy

We saw in Chapter 6 that Parliamentary supremacy is the defining feature of the UK constitution and that (other than in cases of non-compliance with the statutory rule of recognition in s 2(4) of the European Communities Act 1972 (ECA 1972), such as *Factortame*) the courts will not set aside an Act of Parliament.

Judicial review does not enable the courts to strike down Acts of Parliament (the courts can review compatibility with HRA 1998, but there is no power to set aside primary legislation). However, the courts will consider whether executive acts or decisions taken under powers granted via an Act of Parliament have observed the criteria and limitations set by HRA 1998. This includes reviewing the legality of delegated legislation to check whether it exceeds the scope of the law-making powers granted by the relevant enabling Act. Where delegated legislation is found to be illegal, the courts may set it aside (i.e. declare it invalid).

Again, there are differing opinions as to the extent to which judicial review upholds and reinforces the doctrine of Parliamentary sovereignty. On the one hand, the courts can be said to be enforcing the will of Parliament by making Government and other public bodies operate within the statutory limits Parliament has set. On the other hand, the courts have developed judicial review to include the extra-statutory, common law grounds of reasonableness and fairness so that the courts are now judging the legality of public bodies' actions against standards set by the courts themselves, rather than by Parliament. This is particularly so as the courts are placing an increasing emphasis on fundamental common law rights, for example in the *AXA* (2011) case you read about in Chapter 6.

Judicial review and Ministerial accountability

By convention, Government Ministers are accountable to Parliament for the performance of themselves and their departments. As we saw in Chapter 7, this convention has changed over the years, so that 'accountability' now means having to answer Parliamentary questions about the Minister's department rather than necessarily having to take the blame for departmental errors and resign.

Conventions are not legally enforceable and some commentators have questioned the effectiveness of the convention of Ministerial accountability in an electoral system where the House of Commons tends to be dominated by the Government.

Judicial review provides an alternative line of legal (rather than political) accountability, by making Government Ministers and their Departments (as well as other public bodies – see below) answerable to a court of law for their actions and decisions. The threat of a potential claim for judicial review is a strong incentive for Government Departments and other public bodies to act legally, rationally and fairly.

Judicial review – outline

This book is primarily about the UK's constitution and aims to do no more than provide an outline of judicial review. In order to understand the role that judicial review plays within the constitution, you need to understand the procedure by which claims are brought before the courts, the grounds on which they may be brought and the remedies available.

The two-stage structure of a judicial review claim, and some of the key cases, are set out below.

Judicial review – Stage 1: permission to claim

Judicial review is a civil law claim dealt with by the specialist Administrative Court, a division of the High Court. **Part 54 of the Civil Procedure Rules** requires claimants to apply to that court for permission to bring a claim (**Stage 1**) before the substance of the claim can be heard in full (**Stage 2)**. Stage 1 is a filter stage, designed to weed out unmeritorious, frivolous or nuisance claims which may otherwise cause considerable delay and expense to taxpayer-funded public bodies.

There have been some recent reforms to the judicial review process via the **Criminal Justice and Courts Act 2015**. They require that a court may not permit a judicial review to proceed to Stage 2 if it appears 'highly likely' that the decision or action of the public body would not have been substantially different if the conduct complained of had not occurred. They also increase the costs risks to claimants and to third parties (such as charities, representative and pressure groups) that wish to intervene in a judicial review.

These reforms are contentious. 'Red light' theorists are likely to regard them as a dangerous attempt by the Government to exploit its Parliamentary majority to enact reforms that help it to evade the rule of law. 'Green light' theorists, on the other hand, are more likely to see the changes as sensible administrative measures to ensure that the Government is not shackled by, and taxpayers' money is not wasted on defending and hearing, spurious legal challenges.

There are, essentially, seven tests which a claimant must satisfy at Stage 1 in order to persuade the court that the claim deserves to proceed to a full hearing at Stage 2:

1. Is the claim against a public body?
Judicial review may only be claimed against a public body. This is defined as a body (or person) who:

    (a)   gets their powers from legislation; or
    (b)   is exercising prerogative powers (*CCSU* (1984) – see Chapter 7); or
    (c)   is performing a public function (**s 6 HRA 1998** – see Chapter 9; ***Datafin (1987)*** – see below).

KEY CASE: *R (Datafin plc) v Panel on Takeovers and Mergers* [1987] WLR 699

Background:

The Panel was a self-regulating, non-statutory body with exclusive competence to authorise multi-million pound company takeovers in the City of London. Datafin was a company that wished to challenge a decision of the Panel.

Principle:

The Court of Appeal held that although the Panel exercised neither statutory nor prerogative powers (which would have definitively made it a public body), it was performing an important public function which the Government would otherwise have had to discharge. On that basis, it was a public body and amenable to judicial review.

2. Does the claim involve an issue of public law?
The courts will not generally entertain a challenge to a finding of fact made by a public body (e.g. that a house is unfit for human habitation) unless it is totally unsupportable by the evidence (*Coleen Properties Ltd v Minister of Housing and Local Government* (1971) 1 All ER 1049, [1971] 1 WLR 433, CA) or is based on a misinterpretation of the law (*R v Secretary of State for the Home Department ex p Khawaja* (1984) AC 74).

Public bodies engage in a number of private law activities such as contracts, or relationships which give rise to a duty of care. Judicial review is not the appropriate vehicle for a claim based on private law; it is only available in relation to the body's performance of its public functions and where no other private law remedy is available.

3. Does the claim involve a reviewable issue?
As stated above, the courts will not normally review findings of fact, as they consider that the public body (provided it directed itself correctly as to the law) was best placed to evaluate the relevant evidence and considerations.

Nor do the courts traditionally consider themselves competent to review decisions or actions taken under the prerogative which involve matters of 'high policy', such as national security (*CCSU* (1984) – see below; however, note the post-HRA 1998 impact of *A v Secretary of State for the Home Department* (2004)) and decisions to sign international treaties or declarations of war. Respecting the doctrine of the separation of powers, the courts defer to elected politicians on these issues.

Decisions taken under prerogative powers which are administrative in nature and whose impact is limited to particular individuals or groups, as in *ex p Everett* (1989), in which a refusal to issue a passport was successfully challenged, are reviewable.

4. Does the claimant have standing to bring the claim?
In order to protect public bodies from spurious or 'nuisance' challenges, there are rules (in addition to the reforms in the Criminal Justice and Courts Act 2015 outlined above) which restrict the availability of judicial review to those who are actually affected by the action or decision complained of.

Section 31(3) of the Senior Courts Act 1981
The court cannot give permission to proceed with a judicial review claim unless the claimant has a 'sufficient interest' in the matter. The courts have interpreted this to mean either that the claimant must be either directly and adversely affected by the public body's act or decision, or the person or organisation 'best placed' to bring the claim (e.g. a pressure group representing a number of directly affected claimants).

Section 7(3) HRA 1998
Claims alleging breach of Convention rights may be brought by way of judicial review. In these cases, the claimant must show that he is a 'victim' of the alleged breach, i.e. that he himself is directly and adversely affected by it. This rule would appear to exclude pressure groups from bringing human rights challenges. However, in practice, such groups may take part in proceedings as expert witnesses or indirectly by funding the victims' challenges.

5. Are there grounds for review?
To obtain permission to proceed with a claim for judicial review, the claimant must show at Stage 1 that he has arguable and recognised grounds on which the decision may be reviewed. If the claimant gets over this threshold, the case proceeds to a full Stage 2 hearing at which the grounds for review will be considered in detail. While there is considerable overlap between the different grounds for review, the courts have tended to follow the approach taken by Lord Diplock in *CCSU* (1984) and fit them into four categories:

- illegality;
- irrationality (unreasonableness);
- disproportionality;
- unfairness (procedural impropriety).

We will expand upon these grounds below.

6. Last resort?
Judicial review is an option of last resort. It should not be used to short-circuit any statutory appeal or voluntary complaints procedure which is available to the claimant. For criticism of lawyers bringing a premature claim, see *R (Cowl) v Plymouth City Council* (2001) All ER (D) 206 (Dec).

7. Right procedure?
In addition to satisfying all of the tests above, **Part 54 of the Civil Procedure Rules** requires the claim to be brought in the Administrative Court promptly. The outer time limit

is three months from the date that the cause of the claim arose, but this may be restricted further either by statute or by the overriding requirement to be 'prompt'.

Time limits are applied strictly to prevent public bodies incurring delay and unnecessary expense – for example, if you were to wait 11 weeks before deciding to bring a claim to challenge the building of a public road at the end of your garden, the court may well reject your claim at Stage 1 on the grounds that you were not sufficiently 'prompt', particularly if significant public funds have already been spent on the project.

What if the statute excludes judicial review?
In *Anisminic v Foreign Compensation Commission* (1969) 2 AC 147, HL, the courts judicially reviewed a decision of the Commission, despite a clause in the relevant Act which purported to oust their jurisdiction. The House of Lords considered that a decision based on an error of law was a 'nullity', i.e. not a valid decision at all, and that the courts were the exclusive arbiters on all questions of law. The case raises interesting questions about Parliamentary supremacy and judicial assertiveness in defending the rule of law. Even where Parliament appears to have given the executive the right to override a judicial decision, the courts may intervene to restrain them from doing so – see *R (Evans) v Attorney General* (2015) in Chapter 4, in which Lord Neuberger reasserted the principle that it is:

> fundamental to the rule of law that decisions and actions of the executive are…
> reviewable by the court at the suit of an interested citizen.

In 2004, Tony Blair's Labour Government dropped plans to introduce an Act of Parliament excluding the right to judicially review asylum and immigration decisions, in the face of vociferous opposition from the judges and legal profession.[1]

Stage 1: summary
A claimant must satisfy all of the above tests in order to progress to a full hearing of his claim at Stage 2. For a summary of Stage 1, and a handy revision aid for judicial review exam questions, see the **Appendix** to this chapter.

Judicial review – Stage 2: grounds of review

At Stage 2, the court will enquire into the alleged grounds of review in detail. What follows is a summary of the grounds and a handful of key cases.

---

[1] www.telegraph.co.uk/news/1456881/Government- u-turn- on-Asylum- bill.html.

Illegality

In its simplest form, a decision which the public body has no power to make is illegal, however well motivated. The courts call this *ultra vires*, which means simply acting 'outside one's powers'. An example is *Attorney General v Fulham Corporation* (1921), in which the local authority attempted to rely on a power to provide public washing facilities in order to run a paid laundry service. This was held to be *ultra vires* and illegal, despite the popularity of the service.

It remains to be seen how **s 1 of the Localism Act 2011** will affect the doctrine of *ultra vires*. The section gives English local authorities a general power of competence, enabling them to do anything that an individual citizen could legally do. However, the courts have developed the concept of *ultra vires* to include extra-statutory considerations. There is a succession of cases in which, in addition to policing the limits on public bodies' powers expressly laid down in Acts of Parliament, the courts have inferred that Parliament intended those powers to be used properly and in accordance with standards (in effect, set by the judges) of good public administration.

This means that even where a public body has a discretionary power (i.e. a choice) to do something, it is illegal for the body, in reaching its decision, to do any of the following:

Illegal to:	Case	Summary
Fetter its discretion	*R v Secretary of State for Environment ex p Brent LBC* (1982) QB 593, [1983] 3 All ER 321, QBD	The Minister announced that he would reduce the grant paid to the Council prior to consulting it and that there was nothing the Council could say which could make him change his mind.
Ignore relevant considerations	*R v Somerset County Council ex p Fewings* (1995) 3 All ER 20	The Council banned stag hunting on its land. While it was entitled to take into account moral considerations, it had failed to consider its statutory duty to manage the land in the best interests of the area.
Take into account irrelevant considerations	*Padfield v Minister for Agriculture* (1968) 1 All ER 694, HL	The Minister refused to use his power to refer a complaint to a statutory committee, as investigation of the matter would potentially cause him personal embarrassment.
Act for an improper purpose	*Porter v Magill* (2002) 2 AC 357; [2001] UKHL 673, HL	The Westminster 'homes for votes' scandal: the Council Leader used a power to sell Council houses selectively, with houses sold cheaply in areas where she most needed votes.

Just as there is considerable overlap between some of these sub-grounds of illegality (e.g. a decision taken for the wrong purpose will inevitably be based on irrelevant considerations), so there is overlap between illegality and the next ground of review – irrationality.

Irrationality (or unreasonableness)
The courts assume that when Parliament confers powers on public bodies, it intends them to be used rationally. The classic case on irrationality (also known as unreasonableness) is *Wednesbury* (1948):

KEY CASE: *Associated Provincial Picture Houses Ltd v Wednesbury Corporation* **[1948] 1 KB 223**

Background:

Parliament had given the public authority an unlimited statutory discretion to attach conditions to cinema licences. In reliance on this power, the authority had imposed a condition upon a cinema licensed by the authority, banning all children under 15 from attending the cinema on Sundays.

Principle:

A public authority must not exercise its discretion to make a decision which is so unreasonable that no reasonable authority could have made it.

On the facts, the Court of Appeal decided that this particular condition was not so unreasonable (in the moral and social climate of the time!) that no other authority could have imposed it.

This is a test which you will need to know, and be able to apply, in order to be able to answer problem questions on judicial review.

Various judges have rephrased the test for irrationality – e.g. in *CCSU* (1984), Lord Diplock defined an irrational decision as one which:

> is so outrageous in its defiance of logic or accepted moral standards that no sensible person who had applied his mind to the question to be decided would have arrived at it.

The test remains, however, couched in the language of extremes, and is therefore a high threshold for the claimant to cross. Cases are rarely won on this ground alone. Where human rights are in issue, a greater degree of scrutiny is required and the test applied is one of **proportionality**.

Proportionality

After the European Court of Human Rights (the Strasbourg Court) denounced the **Wednesbury** test as inadequate in *Smith v UK* (1999), following the enactment of **HRA 1998** the UK courts recognised that the doctrine of proportionality established through the Strasbourg Court's case law (see Chapter 9) required a more thorough examination of the legitimacy of public bodies' actions where human rights were allegedly infringed.

KEY CASE: *R (Daly) v Secretary of State for the Home Department* [2001] AC 532

Background:

The Home Secretary, in reliance on broad statutory powers to regulate prisons, introduced a new cell search policy in order to tackle a growing problem of drugs being smuggled into prisons. Prison staff were directed to remove the prisoner from the cell while they searched it. They were also directed to examine the prisoner's legal correspondence to check that it did consist of genuine letters to and from his solicitor. D brought a claim for judicial review in order to challenge the lawfulness of the policy, alleging an illegal interference with **Article 8 of the Convention**, which affords a qualified right to private correspondence.

Principle:

Applying the jurisprudence of the European Court of Human Rights, whose decisions UK courts are required to take into account in Convention rights cases by **s 2 HRA 1998**, Lord Steyn formulated a three-stage test to assess whether interference with a qualified Convention right is legal:

    (1)   Is the public body's objective important enough to justify interference?
    (2)   Are the actions taken by the public body rationally connected to that objective?
    (3)   Are the actions no more than necessary to achieve the objective?

On the facts, the House of Lords held that it was unnecessary to exclude non-violent prisoners during searches, and that the blanket nature of the policy was therefore disproportionate and illegal.

In answering problem questions involving interference with a qualified Convention right (see Chapter 9), it is essential that you know, and can apply, the three-stage test in *Daly* (2001).

Some commentators have criticised the different standards applied by the courts in cases involving questions purely of domestic law (the relatively permissive test in *Wednesbury* (1948)) and in cases involving questions of Convention rights (the stricter test in *Daly* (2001)). You will read more in Chapter 9 about the extent to which UK courts are required to take into account decisions of the European Court of Human Rights when interpreting and applying questions of Convention rights.

There has been a succession of recent Supreme Court cases, including *Kennedy v Charity Commission* (2014), *Pham v Secretary of State for the Home Department* (2015) UKSC 19 and *R (Lumsdon) v Legal Services Board* (2015) UKSC 41, in which the Court appears to be moving towards the application of the more structured proportionality test in cases which do not involve questions of EU law or Convention rights. The intensity of the degree to which the Court will scrutinise executive action, e.g. in asking whether it was no more than necessary to achieve the relevant public interest objective, may in future depend on the context, with greater latitude given to the executive in areas which, according to the doctrine of separation of powers, are more appropriately decided by politicians than by judges, e.g. questions of social and economic policy.

Procedural impropriety

Many of the Acts of Parliament conferring powers on public bodies impose particular procedural requirements which must be observed when exercising those powers. Where the public body fails to comply with these statutory rules, it risks its decisions or actions being overturned. This aspect of procedural impropriety is known as 'procedural *ultra vires*' and can be seen as an aspect of Parliamentary supremacy, as it involves the courts enforcing the procedures which Parliament has imposed on executive public bodies.

However, in addition to compliance with any statutory procedural requirements, the courts also expect public bodies to comply with common law principles of 'natural justice'. These are rules which the courts themselves have developed to ensure fairness in dealings between public bodies and the people they serve.

Procedural **ultra vires**

In *R v Immigration Appeal Tribunal ex p Jeyeanthan* (1999) 3 All ER 231, Lord Woolf in the Court of Appeal said that in deciding whether breach of a statutory procedural rule ought to invalidate a public body's decision, the court should consider whether the public body has 'substantially complied' with the rule and, if not, what the consequences of non-compliance are for the claimant.

In that case, the Minister's use of an incorrect form when applying for leave to challenge a grant of asylum did not invalidate the proceedings as it caused no significant prejudice to the other party. The effect of the rule is that failure to dot every procedural 'i' and cross every 't' will not necessarily be fatal to a public body's decision.

Natural justice

The courts have developed certain minimum standards and principles of fairness, with which they expect public bodies to comply in addition to any statutory procedural requirements. These include the right to a fair hearing, the doctrine of legitimate expectations and the rule against bias.

Right to a fair hearing

As a minimum, a fair hearing requires that a person affected by a public body's decision has the right to make representations to the public body about it. This also requires that the person affected is given sufficient notice of any hearing of the matter, and of any allegations against them, to be able to prepare his case and to respond. At the hearing, the public body is under a duty to listen fairly and to give due consideration to each party.

Beyond these basic rules, the requirements of a fair hearing vary according to the context. In cases where the person stands to have something taken from them (as in *Ridge v Baldwin* (1964) AC 40, HL, where a Chief Constable's job was at stake), a fair hearing might require, for example, an oral hearing, the right to legal representation and the right to cross-examine witnesses. In cases where someone is applying for something he does not already have (as in *McInnes v Onslow-Fane* (1978) 3 All ER 211, [1978] 1 WLR 1520, Ch D, where the applicant sought a boxing licence), the matter may be dealt with fairly and adequately without an oral hearing.

Legitimate expectations

Unique to public law, the doctrine of legitimate expectations has been created by the courts to hold public bodies to their promises – even where the public body promised to do something (either expressly or impliedly by a repeated course of conduct) which it was not otherwise obliged to do.

So in *R v Liverpool Corporation ex p Liverpool Taxi Fleet* (1972), the Court of Appeal held that although there was no statutory requirement for the Council to consult existing licence holders before issuing new taxi licences, it was unfair for the Council to disregard its written assurance that it would do so. Any licences issued in the meantime were therefore invalid. In *R v NE Devon Health Authority ex p Coughlan* (2001), the Court of Appeal prohibited the health authority from closing a purpose-built facility at which it had promised the claimant a 'home for life'.

Rule against bias

As we have seen, **Article 6 of the Convention** requires people's civil rights and obligations to be determined by an 'independent and impartial tribunal'. This means that the decision-maker must not be, nor appear to be, biased. Actual bias means that a decision-maker is consciously predisposed to decide a matter in a particular way, whatever the merits of the evidence and the contrary arguments. But the courts are also concerned to avoid 'apparent bias' because public confidence in the administration of justice requires that:

> Justice must not only be done, but must manifestly and undoubtedly be seen to be done.[2]

A decision may be invalidated on the grounds of bias if the decision-maker has any of the following types of interest in the matter under consideration:

Type of interest	Case	Summary
Direct financial interest	*Dimes v Grand Junction Canal Proprietors* (1852)	The court's decision in a long-running matter was set aside as the Lord Chancellor (who had sat in judgment) was found to own shares in the successful party and therefore stood to gain financially from the decision.
Direct non-financial interest	*R v Bow Street Magistrates ex p Pinochet* (1999) 2 WLR 272, HL	The House of Lords' decision to extradite the former Chilean Head of State was set aside as Lord Hoffmann, one of the sitting Law Lords, was a Director of Amnesty International, a party seeking extradition.
Indirect interest	*Porter v Magill* (2002)	The district auditor, M, decided that P was culpable of a deliberate, blatant and dishonest abuse of power and imposed a £20 million surcharge (fine) on her. P appealed on the basis that the auditor had announced his provisional findings at a press conference and was therefore biased. The House of Lords rejected this appeal, holding that 'the question is whether the fair-minded and informed observer, having considered the facts, would conclude that there was a real possibility that the tribunal was biased'.

[2] *R v Sussex Justices ex p McCarthy* [1924] 1 KB 256.

When it comes to answering judicial review problem questions, have confidence in yourself as a 'fair-minded and informed observer'! If you think, having read the facts, that there is a real possibility that the public body (or a key member of it) was biased, then there are grounds to seek one of the remedies set out below.

Judicial review: remedies

The remedies which the court may award on a successful claim for judicial review are set out in **rule 54.2 of the Civil Procedure Rules**. The following remedies are known as **prerogative orders** and are unique to judicial review:

Remedy	Effect	Example
Quashing Order	Renders a public body's decision invalid	*Ex p Pinochet* (2000) – the previous decision of the House of Lords was quashed on the grounds of apparent bias (see above).
Prohibiting Order	Forbids the public body from doing something	*Ex p Liverpool Taxi Fleet* (1972) – the Council was prohibited from issuing more licences until it had consulted existing operators.
Mandatory Order	Forces the public body to do something	*Padfield v Minister of Agriculture* (1968) – the Minister was forced to reconsider the complaint and was directed to take into account those matters which were relevant, and to ignore matters which were irrelevant.

In addition, or as an alternative, to making one of the prerogative orders, the court can make a **declaration**, clarifying the legal position (e.g. in respect of action that the public body proposes to take).

It is important to note that all of the above remedies are discretionary, i.e. the court does not have to award them as of right. Under **s 31(6) of the Senior Courts Act 1981**, the court will balance the interests of the individual claimant against the wider public interest in deciding (a) whether to grant a remedy at all and (b) if so, which remedy is appropriate, and the effect of the **Criminal Justice in Courts Act 2015** is that a claim will not get past Stage 1 if the Court thinks that its outcome will make no substantial difference to the action or decision of the public body.

It is rare to be awarded **damages** on a judicial review. In effect, the claimant has to demonstrate that he would have been entitled to damages in private law, e.g. where a public authority has illegally trespassed on and caused damage to the claimant's land as a result of an unlawful compulsory purchase order.

SUMMARY

- Reforms made by the **Constitutional Reform Act 2005** have separated the judiciary from Parliament and the Government, creating a **Supreme Court** and a **Judicial Appointments Commission**.
- This is important as both **HRA 1998** (in particular, **Article 6 of the Convention**) and the rule of law require an independent judiciary, which can review Government decisions and actions.
- **Judicial review** is the key constitutional interface between Parliament, the Government and the judiciary. While it can be seen as the courts policing the statutory limits set by the democratically elected Parliament, the judges also impose their own standards of reasonableness, fairness and good administration upon public bodies.
- In order to answer a problem question on judicial review, you need to know and be able to apply: (a) the seven tests for obtaining permission to claim (Stage 1); (b) detailed case law on each of the grounds of review – illegality, irrationality, proportionality and procedural impropriety (Stage 2); and (c) the remedies available to a successful claimant.
- You can practise answering judicial review problem questions on the website that accompanies this book. The **Appendix** to this chapter contains a useful flowchart to help you plan and structure your answer.

FURTHER READING

Allan, TRS, 'The constitutional foundations of judicial review: conceptual conundrum or interpretative inquiry?' (2002) *Cambridge Law Journal* 61, 87–125 – this examines the constitutional role of judicial review in light of the doctrines of Parliamentary sovereignty and the rule of law.

Coleman, C, 'Judicial review reform: an attack on our legal rights?' – a brief, but useful and highly readable article by the BBC's legal correspondent on the reforms contained in the Criminal Justice and Courts Act 2015, and their place in the history and evolution of judicial review. Available online at www.bbc.co.uk/news/uk-30226781.

Craig, P, *Administrative Law*, 12th edn, 2012, London: Sweet & Maxwell – probably the leading text book on judicial review: comprehensive, clear and recently updated.

Fordham, M, *Judicial Review Handbook*, 6th edn, 2012, Oxford: Hart – the administrative law practitioner's bible and a treasure trove of case law. If you ever get the chance to see Michael Fordham speaking, whether in court (he's a leading public law barrister) or at a conference, take it – he's brilliant.

http://ukscblog.com/case-comment-r-lumsdon-ors-v-legal-services-board-2015-uksc-41 – case comment by David Hart QC on the Supreme Court decision in *R (Lumsdon) v Legal Services*

Board (2015) and the differing standards of review adopted by the Court when applying the proportionality test depending on whether the case involves EU law or Convention rights.

www.telegraph.co.uk/news/uknews/1456043/Law-lords-raise-stakes-on-asylum.html – a report by Joshua Rozenberg on adverse judicial reaction to the Home Secretary's inclusion of a clause in the Asylum and Immigration Bill (2004) seeking to prevent the courts from judicially reviewing executive decisions in that field – the clause was eventually abandoned.

COMPANION WEBSITE

An online glossary compiled by the author is available on the companion website: www. routledge.com/cw/beginningthelaw

Judicial Review – Outline of a Claim: Stage 1

Is the defendant a public body?	**No** →	
↓ Yes		If the answer to any one or more of these questions is 'no', then the claim for judicial review fails.
Does the claim involve an issue of public law?	**No** →	
↓ Yes		*Note that the court will, at the initial stage, only consider whether or not there appear to be arguable grounds for review. If so, the court may grant the claimant permission to proceed with the claim.
Is it a reviewable issue?	**No** →	
↓ Yes		
Does the claimant have standing to bring the claim?	**No** →	
↓ Yes		
Are there grounds for review?*	**No** →	
↓ Yes		If permission is granted, the claim proceeds to a full hearing where the grounds for review will be considered in detail.
Is judicial review being claimed as a last resort?	**No** →	
↓ Yes		
Has the claimant followed the right procedure?	**No** →	
↓ Yes		

TURN OVER – GO TO STAGE 2

<u>Judicial Review – Detailed Grounds of Argument: Stage 2</u>

Applying the relevant grounds of review identified by LJ Diplock in CCSU

<u>Illegality</u>	<u>Irrationality</u>	<u>Procedural impropriety</u>
Has the public body: • exceeded its powers? Or abused its powers e.g.: • fettered its discretion? • acted for an improper purpose? • acted on irrelevant considerations? and/or • ignored relevant considerations? NB: you will need to back up your arguments with cases.	Has the public body: • acted so unreasonably that no public body could have acted like that *(Wednesbury)*? or • acted in a way that is illogical, outrageous or perverse *(CCSU)*? NB: if specific human rights are infringed, consider: <u>Proportionality</u> i.e. is the interference: • legally authorised? • rationally connected to a legitimate aim? • no more than necessary *(Daly)*?	Has the public body: • substantially failed to comply with a procedural rule in the relevant statute *(Jeyeanthan)*? Or breached the rules of natural justice, i.e.: • the right to a fair hearing *(Ridge v Baldwin)*? and/or • the rule against bias – would the reasonable person think there was a real possibility of bias *(Porter v Magill)*?

<u>Remedies</u> Consider whether the claim is likely to succeed on any of the above grounds. Advise whether one or more of the following remedies are appropriate: Quashing Order/Mandatory Order/Prohibiting Order/Declaration (NB: no right to damages unless under s 8 HRA 1998, or private law).

Chapter 9

Human Rights Act 1998 and the European Convention on Human Rights

LEARNING OBJECTIVES

After reading this chapter, you should be able to:

- Explain how the Human Rights Act 1998 (HRA 1998) incorporates the European Convention on Human Rights (the Convention) into UK law
- Understand the difference between absolute rights and qualified (or limited) rights
- Analyse the proportionality of alleged interferences of Convention rights
- Apply the definition of a 'public authority' in s 6 HRA 1998.

INTRODUCTION

In Chapter 6 we discussed the impact of HRA 1998's incorporation of Convention rights into UK law on the relationship between Parliament and the courts. In Chapter 8 we considered how HRA 1998 has impacted on the relationship between the courts and the Government.

In this chapter we examine HRA 1998's impact on the citizen. We will begin with an appraisal of the Convention rights which HRA 1998 imports, and the jurisprudence underlying them, before moving on to consider how the key provisions of HRA 1998 protect the citizen against interference with those rights by public authorities.

THE EUROPEAN CONVENTION ON HUMAN RIGHTS

The Convention was drafted as a response to Nazi atrocities carried out during World War II. UK lawyers and civil servants were heavily involved in its drafting. It aimed to protect 'fundamental rights and freedoms' by giving citizens who believed that these rights had been infringed the right to complain to the European Court of Human Rights in Strasbourg, France.

The Convention was ratified by the UK in 1951 and came into force in 1953, but was not incorporated by Parliament into domestic law. This meant that a UK citizen who felt that his Convention rights had been unlawfully infringed by the Government had to take the case to Strasbourg to seek a declaration that the Government had acted unlawfully – this was time-consuming and expensive.

THE EUROPEAN COURT OF HUMAN RIGHTS

The Convention is drafted in a very different way from domestic UK statutes. Rather than specifying every single set of circumstances in which a particular right can be restricted, it lays down broad principles to assist the courts in balancing individual rights against the wider public interest when deciding whether these rights have been unlawfully infringed.

The European Court of Human Rights is referred to in this chapter as 'the Strasbourg Court'. It is established by Article 19 of the Convention and is responsible for holding the 47 states that have signed up to the Convention to account for their implementation and observance of the Convention rights. Each of the signatory States nominates three candidates from which a judge representing that State is chosen to serve a non-renewable nine-year term of office.

As discussed in Chapter 6, **s 2 HRA 1998** provides that UK courts are not required to follow decisions of the Strasbourg Court in deciding whether Convention rights have been unlawfully infringed. They are, however, required to take account of decisions of the Strasbourg Court, and so it is important to understand the jurisprudence of the Strasbourg Court, i.e. the key principles underpinning its decisions.

The Strasbourg Court has stressed that the Convention is a 'living instrument'. This means that as society and attitudes change, the Strasbourg Court will change and develop the way in which it interprets the Convention. Rights may be extended and protected to cover situations not necessarily envisaged when the original Convention was drafted. The Strasbourg Court tends to focus on the spirit rather than the letter of the Convention rights. This is known as **purposive** or **teleological** interpretation.

The Strasbourg Court, however, still tends to follow the precedents it has set in earlier cases – where it does not, it will make it clear why it is not doing so. It is therefore important to look at past decisions of the Strasbourg Court in analysing how it is likely to view any new cases. It is also crucially important to be clear at the outset of a matter as to which Convention rights are engaged and what sort of rights they are.

'Absolute' rights

The substance of the rights and freedoms enshrined in the Convention is set out in a series of Articles. Some Convention rights are absolute – i.e. the Convention **permits no interference with them by the State in any circumstances.** An example is:

Article 3, European Convention on Human Rights

No one shall be subjected to torture or to inhuman or degrading treatment or punishment.

This Article gives no scope for State interference – any State involvement in torture is illegal.

Other rights may contain some express, specific exceptions, but are still considered to be 'absolute'. An example is **Article 4**, which contains an absolute prohibition on slavery and forced labour, but makes a specific exception for compulsory military service (which, until 2011, was still required in Germany). Despite this, Article 4 is still considered an absolute right as it gives national Governments no *general* power to force their citizens to work.

'Qualified' or 'limited' rights

Other rights are 'qualified' or 'limited' because they can lawfully be restricted in the circumstances set out in the relevant Article. Typically, qualified or limited rights have a two-part structure, in which paragraph 1 sets out the basic right or freedom and paragraph 2 then qualifies it by setting out the circumstances in which the right may be limited. For example:

Article 8, European Convention on Human Rights

1. Everyone has the right to respect for his private and family life, his home and his correspondence.
2. There shall be no interference by a public authority with the exercise of this right except such as is in accordance with the law and is necessary in a democratic society in the interests of national security, public safety or the economic well-being of the country, for the prevention of disorder or crime, for the protection of health or morals, or for the protection of the rights and freedoms of others.

These rights fundamentally differ from, for example, Article 4 because the list of situations in which they may lawfully be restricted is not closed. There is a general scope for interference where the public authority can demonstrate that interference is:

- in accordance with the law; and
- necessary in a democratic society…
- … in the interests of one or more of the public policy aims set out in the Article.

'In accordance with the law'

There has to be a clear legal basis for the restriction imposed by the relevant State's own domestic law. As far as the UK is concerned, this would require a clear and unambiguous statutory power for the relevant government body to impose the restriction.

KEY CASE: *Halford v UK* [1997] 24 EHRR 523

Background:

H, the Assistant Chief Constable of Merseyside Police, alleged that her office phone had been unlawfully tapped by her employers. Because the Interception of Communications Act 1985 did not regulate the surveillance of internal telephone networks, she had no remedy in domestic law.

Principle:

The Strasbourg Court held that in the absence of adequate regulation in domestic UK law, the phone tapping was an unlawful interference with the applicant's Article 8 right to privacy.

As a result of the Strasbourg Court's decision in *Halford* (1997), the **Regulation of Investigatory Powers Act 2000** was passed.

On-the-spot question

 Which of the important constitutional concepts which we examined in Chapter 4 does the decision in *Halford v UK* (1997) and the subsequent enactment of the Regulation of Investigatory Powers Act 2000 reflect?

'Necessary in a democratic society'

The Strasbourg Court has developed two key concepts to aid its interpretation of whether or not a particular restriction is necessary for the pursuance of a legitimate aim.

Proportionality

Most questions before the Strasbourg Court require the Court to strike a 'fair balance' between the rights of the individual and the wider public policy aim relied on by the State to justify interference.

The concept of proportionality requires the State to demonstrate that the methods it has chosen in order to achieve its legitimate aim go no further than is absolutely necessary. There must be a rational and clear link between the measures taken and the purpose to be achieved. Any interference which goes beyond that which is absolutely necessary is **disproportionate** and therefore unlawful (even where it is prescribed by law and stated to be in pursuance of a legitimate aim).

The key question when examining whether a particular restriction is disproportionate is: could the State have achieved the relevant, legitimate aim without restricting Convention rights in this way?

We saw in Chapter 8 how the UK courts applied the doctrine of proportionality in deciding that the Home Secretary's blanket exclusion of prisoners during cell searches was unlawful in *Daly* (2001). In the more recent case of *Bank Mellat* (2013), the Supreme Court has added a fourth dimension to the test for whether a particular interference with a Convention right is proportionate:

KEY CASE: *Bank Mellat v HM Treasury* **[2013] UKSC 39**

Background:

HM Treasury issued an Order using powers under the Counter-Terrorism Act 2008, preventing Bank Mellat, an Iranian bank, from doing business in the UK. The Treasury said that the bank had connections with Iran's nuclear and ballistic missile programme, and so the Order was made on national security grounds.

Decision:

A nine-judge Supreme Court held by a majority of 5:4 that the Order was arbitrary, irrational and disproportionate. The risk of the bank's facilities being used in connection with nuclear proliferation was an inherent risk of banking, and the Treasury had failed to justify the singling out of Bank Mellat. The Order was therefore an unlawful interference with the bank's business property rights under Article 1, Protocol 1 of the Convention and was struck down.

Principle:

Lord Reed set out a four-stage test for assessing whether interference with a qualified or limited Convention right is proportionate, adding an additional consideration to the three-stage test set out in *Daly* (2001). The questions that the Court must ask are:

(1)   whether the objective of the measure is sufficiently important to justify the limitation of a protected right,
(2)   whether the measure is rationally connected to the objective,
(3)   whether a less intrusive measure could have been used without unacceptably compromising the achievement of the objective, and
(4)   whether the severity of the measure's impact on people's rights outweighs its contribution to the public interest objective.

The majority differed from the minority in the relative weight to be given to rights under Article 1, Protocol 1 when set against the public interest in taking precautionary action to prevent nuclear proliferation.

On-the-spot question

Why do you think that the Supreme Court has added this additional step into the assessment of proportionality? What are the difficulties for the Court in applying steps 3 and 4 – do you think that these questions should be answered by judges or by politicians?

Margin of discretion

This concept was developed by the Strasbourg Court in order to recognise and accommodate national and local differences in political, religious and moral customs and practices.

The Strasbourg Court will not substitute its own moral views for those of the relevant State. It confines itself to asking whether the relevant State was reasonably entitled to think that its interference with a qualified right was justifiable and proportionate in light of local conditions.

KEY CASE: *Otto-Preminger Institute v Austria* (1995) 19 EHRR 34

Background:

The complainants ran a cinema. They wanted to show a film critical of the Catholic religion which, among other things, portrayed Christ as mentally defective. The Austrian authorities confiscated the film. The institute complained that this was an unlawful interference with their **Article 10(1)** right to freedom of expression.

Principle:

The Strasbourg Court held that the confiscation was:

- **prescribed by law** – Austrian law gave the State the necessary powers of seizure;
- **in pursuance of a legitimate public policy aim** – there was evidence that there could be riots if the film were shown, and the prevention of public disorder was recognised by **Article 10(2)** as a legitimate ground for interference;
- **proportionate** – as 87 per cent of the local population (in the Tyrol region, where the film was to be shown) was Catholic, the Strasbourg Court considered it **within Austria's margin of appreciation** to consider the confiscation '**necessary**' to prevent disorder.

On-the-spot question

Do you think that the *Otto-Preminger* (1995) case would have been decided the same way had the cinema which wanted to show the film been located in London?

Non-discrimination

Article 14, European Convention on Human Rights

The enjoyment of the rights and freedoms set forth in this Convention shall be secured without discrimination on any ground such as sex, race, colour, language, religion, political or other opinion, national or social origin, association with a national minority, property, birth or other status.

In addition to being in accordance with the law, and proportionate to a recognised public policy aim, interference with Convention rights must not be based on a discriminatory factor such as race, nationality, gender or sexuality. Article 14 does not confer a stand-alone right not to be discriminated against, but does assist those who wish to argue that another of their Convention rights has been restricted by a measure applied only to a particular group.

HRA 1998

HRA 1998 incorporates the following Convention rights into domestic law:

Article 2	Right to life
Article 3	Prohibition of torture, or inhuman or degrading treatment or punishment
Article 4	Prohibition of slavery and forced labour
Article 5	Right to liberty and security
Article 6	Right to a fair trial
Article 7	No punishment without law
Article 8	Right to respect for private and family life
Article 9	Freedom of thought, conscience and religion
Article 10	Freedom of expression
Article 11	Freedom of assembly and association
Article 12	Right to marry
Article 14	Prohibition of discrimination
Article 1, Protocol 1	Protection of property, peaceful enjoyment of possessions
Article 2, Protocol 1	Right to education
Article 3, Protocol 1	Right to free elections

The practical effect of this on the citizen is that anyone in the UK can now bring claims that these Convention rights have been infringed in their national (and local) courts – this is less costly and less time-consuming than having to take a case to the Strasbourg Court.

How does HRA 1998 incorporate Convention rights?

Section 1 provides that the Convention Articles listed in Schedule 1 HRA 1998 are to have effect (i.e. be directly enforceable) subject to any derogations. A **derogation** is a temporary opt-out measure under **Article 15** of the Convention, available to national Governments only in times of 'war or other public emergency threatening the life of the nation'. We saw in Chapter 6 how the UK derogated from Article 5 in the immediate period following the 9/11 attacks.

Section 2 makes European Court of Human Rights judgments persuasive in arguments before UK courts, which must take account of them, but it does not *require* UK courts to follow the Strasbourg Court.

In *R v Horncastle* (2009) UKSC 14, the Supreme Court declined to follow the Strasbourg Court's ruling in *Al-Khawaja v UK* (2009) that Article 6 of the Convention precludes the conviction of a defendant charged with a criminal offence solely on the strength of hearsay evidence. Lord Phillips said that, while the Supreme Court normally follows the Strasbourg Court:

> there are occasions where this court has concerns as to whether a decision of the Strasbourg Court sufficiently appreciates or accommodates particular aspects of our domestic process. In such circumstances it is open to this court to decline to follow the Strasbourg decision, giving reasons for adopting this course.

Section 3 requires all legislation (primary and secondary) to be read and given effect in a way which is compatible with the Convention rights (whether or not it was enacted before HRA 1998 came into force), so far as it is possible to do so. The impact of this provision on Parliamentary sovereignty was discussed in Chapter 6, where you read about the controversial decision in *R v A* (2001).

Section 4 empowers the courts to declare an Act of Parliament to be incompatible with Convention rights – a **'declaration of incompatibility'**. As we saw in Chapter 6, where you read about *A v Secretary of State for the Home Department* (2004), such a declaration does *not* affect the legal validity of the Act, which continues in force until and unless amended or repealed by Parliament. Note that while the courts cannot set aside primary legislation under HRA 1998, they *can* set aside any secondary legislation which unlawfully contravenes the Convention rights incorporated by Schedule 1 of HRA

1998 (see the discussion on **judicial review** in Chapter 8 and the ***Bank Mellat* (2013)** case above).

Section 19 requires the Government Minister who introduces a Bill into Parliament to make a statement as to the Bill's compatibility with Convention rights. Such a statement is not binding on the courts; it merely sets out the Government's view as to compatibility, and is intended mainly to identify whether Parliament is being invited to legislate deliberately and consciously in a way which is incompatible with the Convention.

What obligations do public authorities have under HRA 1998?

Section 6 makes it unlawful for a '**public authority**' to act incompatibly with Convention rights unless forced to do so by primary legislation.

'**Public authority**' includes a court or tribunal and any person or organisation '**whose functions are of a public nature**' – it does not include either House of Parliament (or their members, when acting in their legislative capacity).

This definition has generated much litigation. While it is clear that some organisations (e.g. local councils, NHS trusts and police forces) are public authorities, the situation is less clear where a private organisation (e.g. a limited company) is arguably carrying out public functions. Such organisations can be a private body in one context and a public authority in another: a 'hybrid' public authority.

Some of the case law can be difficult to reconcile, and while factors such as public funding and a direct delegation of powers to the private body may tend towards it being a public authority, it is important to consider all the circumstances.

> **KEY CASE:** *R (Beer) v Hampshire Farmers' Markets Ltd* [2003] EWCA Civ 1056
>
> Background:
>
> A private limited company was formed and supported by the local Council to run markets (previously run by the Council itself) on Council-owned land.
>
> Principle:
>
> In relation to its licensing of market stallholders, the company was carrying out a public function and was therefore a public authority with a duty to comply with Convention rights.

KEY CASE: *YL v Birmingham City Council* [2007] UKHL 27

Background:

The appellant was a resident at a care home run by a private company. Her placement had been arranged by the Council pursuant to its statutory healthcare duties. The Council part-funded the placement and had in effect sub-contracted its functions to the company.

Principle:

Despite this, the House of Lords (by a majority of 3:2) decided that the company was not, in this context, a public authority. It was important to consider the need to treat privately funded and State-funded residents equally.

KEY CASE: *Aston Cantlow Parochial Church Council v Wallbank* **[2003] UKHL 37**

Background:

W bought a farm which carried with it an obligation in property law to maintain a church roof. The Parochial Church Council (part of the Church of England) went to court to enforce W's obligation to pay for repairs. W claimed under s 6 HRA 1998 that this was a disproportionate interference with their right to peaceful enjoyment of their possessions under Article 1, Protocol 1 of the Convention. The success of their claim depended on whether the Parochial Church Council was a 'public authority'.

Principle:

The House of Lords held that while the Church of England was a public authority when performing activities which could be considered 'public functions', e.g. marriages and funerals, in this context it was merely enforcing a private property law right like any other landowner and was not therefore a 'public authority' for the purposes of the claim.

Section 7 provides that where a public authority has acted (or failed to act) contrary to section 6 (i.e. incompatibly with Convention rights), anyone who is a **'victim'** of (i.e. is directly and adversely affected by) the act or omission can bring legal proceedings against the public authority, or can rely on their Convention right in their own defence.

Section 8 empowers the courts to award any remedy within their powers where a public authority has breached Convention rights – this might include:

* damages (i.e. compensation);
* an injunction (to force the authority to do, or not to do, something); and/or
* a 'Quashing' Order (see Chapter 8).

Possible repeal of HRA 1998

You read in Chapter 6 about proposals to repeal HRA 1998. We said that those proposals raise some important questions, such as:

* Will the UK withdraw from the Convention?
* Will the UK withdraw from the EU, whose Charter of Fundamental Rights largely replicates key Convention rights?
* What will happen to human rights in Scotland and Wales, where the Convention is hard-wired into the devolution settlements?
* How might the UK judges, who are increasingly using the common law to protect and assert fundamental rights, react to the repeal of HRA 1998?

As we said in Chapter 6, it is important that you follow the debate in the news as to whether HRA 1998 should be repealed and, if so, what will replace it.

In the meantime, now that you understand more about the way that the Strasbourg Court and the UK courts interpret and protect Convention rights, you might find it useful to think some more about the questions set out above. The **Further reading** set out below will help you to do that.

SUMMARY

* HRA 1998 requires public authorities to comply with the rights and freedoms of the Convention, which can be enforced in UK courts.
* HRA 1998 imports key doctrines such as proportionality and purposive interpretation into UK law, and has had a profound impact on the way in which domestic courts protect citizens' rights, and the degree of judicial scrutiny to

which laws and executive decisions are subject, although UK courts are not bound to follow the decisions of the European Court of Human Rights.

- The Government currently proposes to repeal HRA 1998. It will be important for you to keep up with the news on this important constitutional issue.

FURTHER READING

Fenwick, H, 'What's wrong with s.2 of the Human Rights Act?', UK Constitutional Law Blog (9 October 2012), available at http://ukconstitutionallaw.org – a fascinating article on the relationship between the Strasbourg Court and the UK courts

Hart, D, 'An ABC on proportionality – with Bank Mellat as our primer', UK Human Rights Blog (22 June 2013), available at http://ukhumanrightsblog.com – as the title of the article suggests, this is an accessible, entry-level discussion of the doctrine of proportionality, which is fundamental to understanding Convention rights

Sankey, B, 'Legally illiterate' (2 October 2014), available at www.liberty-human-rights.org.uk/news/blog/legally-illiterate – an article by Liberty's Director of Policy, criticising the policy behind the Government's proposed repeal of HRA 1998. You should be aware that this is a political article and give it appropriate weight – but it does address some of the legal difficulties around repeal of HRA 1998, such as the relationship with the Convention and the Strasbourg Court, and the impact on the devolution settlements.

COMPANION WEBSITE

An online glossary compiled by the author is available on the companion website: www.routledge.com/cw/beginningthelaw

Chapter 10
Police powers and public order

LEARNING OBJECTIVES

After reading this chapter, you should be able to:

- Understand how, within the context of the Convention rights, the Police and Criminal Evidence Act 1984 (PACE 1984) imposes specific restrictions on police powers
- Consider the impact of the Human Rights Act 1998 (HRA 1998) on the policing of public demonstrations under the Public Order Act 1986
- Know how to answer exam questions about PACE 1984 and the Public Order Act 1986.

INTRODUCTION

In Chapter 9 we began with an appraisal of the rights under the European Convention on Human Rights (the Convention) and the jurisprudence underlying them, before moving on to consider how HRA 1998 has fundamentally changed the culture of rights in the UK. In this chapter we continue to examine the impact of HRA 1998 on the citizen in the context of Article 5 (right to liberty), Article 6 (right to a fair trial), Article 10 (freedom of expression) and Article 11 (freedom of assembly and association) of the Convention.

Particular attention will be paid to police powers under PACE 1984 and restrictions on the right to protest under the Public Order Act 1986. These are favourite topics of examiners, and this chapter explains how to apply the key provisions in answering a problem question.

HRA 1998 AND FREEDOM OF THE PERSON

Freedom of the person in the UK (as in all other countries) is not absolute. A person's liberty may be restricted by police powers of stop, search, arrest and detention, and by imprisonment under the criminal justice system.

The legal context for deprivation of liberty in the UK is conditioned by Articles 5 and 6 of the Convention. We will consider the scope of the rights protected by these Articles and the extent to which the Convention permits them to be restricted. We will then consider how these restrictions manifest themselves in UK law by examining some key provisions of PACE 1984 and case law applying those provisions.

Article 5: the right to liberty

This Article seeks to ensure freedom from arbitrary arrest and detention. A State may detain someone only 'in accordance with a procedure prescribed by law' and in pursuance of specified objectives (see **Article 5(1)(a)–(f)**), which include arrest in order to bring a suspect before a court, and detention after conviction.

Article 5(2)–(5) sets out procedural rights for the person arrested:

- to be informed promptly of the arrest;
- to be brought to court promptly and receive a trial within a reasonable time;
- to test the legality of detention before a court;
- to compensation for breach of Article 5.

Article 6: the right to a fair trial

Each citizen has the right to a fair and public hearing by an independent and impartial tribunal in determination of any criminal charge against them.

KEY CASE: *Khan v UK* (2001) 31 EHRR 45

Background:

K had made several admissions of involvement in illegal drugs importation while unknowingly being recorded on an electronic listening device. He pleaded guilty, then appealed, challenging the admissibility of the evidence. K argued that since the tape-recordings were in breach of Article 8, their admissibility violated Article 6(1).

Principle:

The European Court of Human Rights (the Strasbourg Court) held that under Article 8(1) the surveillance was not in accordance with the law as at the time there was no domestic law covering this. However, it was for the UK courts to decide whether the illegally obtained evidence ought to be ruled admissible at trial – see **s 78 PACE 1984** (below).

Police surveillance is now regulated by the **Regulation of Investigatory Powers Act 2000 (RIPA 2000)**.

PACE 1984

PACE 1984 was passed in order to codify and set limits on police powers, after allegations of institutional racism and persecution of ethnic minorities led to widespread rioting in the UK's inner cities. It remains the main source of police powers over 30 years later.

While it is not possible in a book of this size to give a comprehensive analysis of PACE 1984, which contains 122 sections and schedules, what follows is an overview of some of the provisions most likely to crop up in examination questions. Typically these questions require you to apply the provisions of PACE 1984 to a problem scenario and advise whether the police have acted lawfully.

PACE 1984: powers of arrest

Section 24 gives the police the power to arrest without warrant (i.e. an on-the-spot arrest which does not require prior authorisation by a court) where the following conditions are met:

- the police officer has **reasonable grounds to suspect** that the person arrested has committed, is committing or is about to commit a criminal offence; and
- it is **necessary** to arrest the suspect for one or more of the reasons in **s 24(5)** – e.g. to prevent someone being harmed, to prevent property damage, to stop the suspect from getting away or to facilitate the investigation of the offence.

In addition, for the arrest to be lawful, **s 28** requires the officer to inform the suspect as soon as practicable both that they are being arrested and the reason why they are being arrested (i.e. the specific offence they are suspected of having committed). It may not be practicable to give this information immediately upon arrest, particularly if a struggle ensues, but once the suspect is subdued and under police control, the arrest is unlawful until it is given (*Director of Public Prosecutions v Hawkins* (1988)).

PACE 1984: powers ancillary to arrest

Section 17 permits an officer to enter private property to make an arrest for an **indictable offence** – i.e. one for which the suspect could, if charged, be tried by a jury in a Crown Court (this includes most offences involving theft and/or violence).

Section 117 is a general power for the police to use **reasonable force** when exercising any of their powers under PACE 1984. This requires consideration of whether force is necessary at all and, if so, whether the degree of force used is proportionate.

PACE 1984: detention at the police station

On arrival at the police station (which should be as soon as possible after arrest – **s 30**), a **custody officer** is responsible for taking the suspect's details, searching them to record (and, where the grounds in **s 54(4)** permit, confiscate) their possessions and deciding whether or not to detain them. There are two permitted grounds for detention:

- to **secure or preserve evidence relating to the offence for which the suspect is under arrest** (e.g. by searching the suspect's premises – see below); or
- to **obtain such evidence by questioning.**

The initial maximum period for which the suspect can be detained is 24 hours (**s 41**). In the case of an indictable offence, **ss 42–44** provide for gradual extensions of this time limit up to a maximum of 96 hours. This is subject to review after an initial 6 hours, and then every 9 hours, by an officer not involved in the investigation, to check that grounds for detention still exist. Failure to carry out the reviews renders subsequent detention unlawful (*Roberts v Chief Constable of Cheshire* (1999)).

PACE 1984: key rights of the suspect at the police station

Section 56 entitles a suspect to have one friend or relative told, as soon as practicable, that he is being detained at the police station. In the case of an indictable offence, an **inspector** can delay the exercise of this right for a maximum of 36 hours if he **reasonably believes** that notification will lead to evidence being interfered with, people being harmed, other suspects being alerted or property being spirited away.

Section 58 gives suspects the right to free and independent legal advice. A duty solicitor rota operates so that solicitors are 'on call' to attend upon and advise suspects detained at a police station. The right to legal advice can only be delayed in the case of an indictable offence and on similar grounds to those in **s 56** (above). Under s 58, however, the decision to delay must be taken by a **superintendent** (or higher-ranking officer). This reflects the importance of this fundamental right.

On-the-spot question

? Consider the grounds on which the right to free and independent legal advice can be delayed under **s 58 PACE 1984**. If you were a duty solicitor and you became aware that a suspect had not been allowed to contact you for advice because a superintendent considered that one or more of these grounds applied, how would you feel? What does the superintendent's decision imply?

PACE 1984: charge or release?

When the police have sufficient evidence to charge the arrested person, he must be charged or released. If the suspect is charged, he must be brought before the next session of the magistrates' court, or released, usually on bail to appear at the magistrates' court – **ss 38 and 46**. As a general rule, there is no power to continue to question a person about an offence once they have been charged.

PACE 1984: search and entry powers

The police have an array of powers to search people, and to enter and search premises. A brief summary is set out below:

Section	Power	Conditions
1	To stop and search people and vehicles in a public place.	Reasonable belief that the officer will find stolen or prohibited items.
8	To request a search warrant from the magistrates' court.	Indictable offences only.
17	To enter premises to arrest a suspect, execute a search or arrest warrant or 'save life and limb'.	Indictable offences only.
18	To search premises following arrest for evidence related to that or related offences.	Indictable offences only. Must be authorised in writing by an inspector.
19	To seize and retain (**s 22**) evidence relating to *any* offence where necessary.	The officer must be lawfully on the premises (e.g. in execution of a search warrant or in pursuance of a duly authorised search under s 18).
32	To search a suspect upon arrest.	Reasonable belief that the suspect is dangerous, might escape or has evidence in relation to an offence.
54	Custody Officer's power to search suspect on arrival at police station.	Can seize items on grounds in **s 54(4)**, provided the suspect is told why they have been seized.

The police can use reasonable and necessary force (**s 117**) in the lawful exercise of any of the search and entry powers set out above.

PACE 1984: remedies

Where the police fail to comply with the conditions on the exercise of their PACE 1984 powers, remedies include:

- Damages for unlawful detention (false imprisonment). In *Thompson v MPC* (1997), the court set a tariff of £500 for the first hour of unlawful detention and £3,000 for 24 hours. Additional, exemplary damages can be awarded where the police misconduct is malicious or particularly blameworthy.
- Damages for trespass to goods (e.g. property damage during an illegal search).
- Damages for trespass to the person (e.g. an assault by the unlawful use of force).
- Habeas corpus: a special application to court that requires the police to justify the lawfulness of detaining the suspect.
- Judicial review of, for example, an illegally issued search warrant.
- A complaint to the **Independent Police Complaints Commission (IPCC)**. The IPCC is funded by the Home Office, but is by law entirely independent of the police, interest groups and political parties, and its decisions on cases are free from government involvement. It has a legal duty to oversee the whole of the police complaints system. It can choose to manage or supervise the police investigation into a case, and can independently investigate the most serious cases (e.g. police shootings such as that of John Charles de Menezes in July 2005). Part of the IPCC's remit is to increase public confidence in the police.

PACE 1984: exclusion of evidence

In addition to the above remedies, the more serious consequence (for both the police and the suspect) of a breach of PACE 1984 may be the impact on the admissibility of unlawfully gathered evidence at trial. There are two key provisions you need to know.

Section 78: unfair evidence

Evidence may still be admissible at trial even when it has been illegally obtained. However, the court has a **general discretion** to exclude such evidence where to admit it would have **such an adverse effect on the fairness of proceedings that the court ought not to do so**.

> **KEY CASE: *Watson v Director of Public Prosecutions* [2003] EWHC 1466**
>
> Background:
>
> The defendant to a drink-driving charge had made an oral admission to the police that he was the driver of a car involved in an accident. Although the police officer

had failed to comply with the relevant PACE Code of Practice by not making a note of the admission at the time, the defendant had a reasonable opportunity to deny that he was the driver, and there was no suggestion of bad faith by the arresting officer.

Principle:

The magistrates were entitled under **s 78** to allow the admission to be used in evidence at the defendant's trial.

Section 76: confessions

A confession is defined by **s 82** as any statement which is wholly or partly adverse to the party who made it. If the defence represent that a confession is **unreliable** or was obtained by **oppression**, the court **must exclude it unless the prosecution proves otherwise**.

KEY CASE: *R v Paris, Abdullahi & Miller* [1993] 97 Cr App R 99

Background:

M was charged with the murder of a prostitute. The main evidence against M was his confession evidence, which was ruled admissible at trial. M and two other defendants (P and A) implicated by M's confession were later convicted of murder. All three appealed on the ground that the confession had been obtained in oppressive circumstances which rendered it unreliable. M was borderline mentally disabled and had been interviewed for 13 hours, during which he denied involvement over 300 times. The police had made it clear to M that they would continue to question him until they 'got it right'. Although M's solicitor was present, he did little to intervene.

Principle:

The Court of Appeal held that the confession was clearly unreliable and should not have been admitted. The jury might have been prejudiced by that confession evidence against the other appellants, and so those convictions were also unsafe and unsatisfactory and would also be quashed. The Court of Appeal were critical of the duty solicitor: 'In our view, although we do not know what instructions he had, the solicitor appears to have been gravely at fault for sitting passively through this travesty of an interview.'

PACE 1984: exam tips

Examination questions on PACE 1984 usually take the form of a problem scenario, containing a number of possible breaches of the Act's provisions. Some examiners let you take in a statute book containing the relevant provisions; others require you to learn them. Even where you have a statute book, you need to be sufficiently familiar with the key provisions as you will not have much time to read them in the exam!

Keeping a cool head and approaching the question in a methodical way are important. Here is a suggested plan which I have nicknamed the '**DIA-GRAM**':

1. **D**efine each relevant event of police procedure (e.g. search, arrest, detention).
2. **I**dentify the relevant PACE 1984 provisions and the key tests or conditions they contain (e.g. reasonable suspicion, necessity).
3. **A**pply those provisions to the facts, checking that each relevant condition for the exercise of the power is satisfied.
4. **G**ive a **R**easoned **A**nd **M**easured conclusion as to whether the exercise of the power is lawful; if not, then **consider the effect of this on the admissibility of evidence** at trial and what **remedies** may be available to the client.

HRA 1998 AND FREEDOM OF ASSEMBLY

In a democracy, the right to stage public protests is important. It is also important that this right is balanced with powers to police public demonstrations so as to prevent threats to public safety and damage to property. Both the Convention and the Public Order Act 1986 attempt to strike this balance (more 'amber light' solutions). The key Convention rights are set out in Articles 10 and 11.

Article 10: freedom of expression

This is a qualified right, balancing the right to freedom of expression and the right 'to receive and impart information and ideas' with:

> such formalities, conditions, restrictions and penalties as are prescribed by law and are necessary in a democratic society, in the interests of national security... public safety... the prevention of disorder or crime... [and] the protection of the... rights of others.

Article 11: freedom of assembly and association

The right to freedom of assembly and association is subject to lawful restrictions by the police, on similar public interest grounds as set out above in relation to **Article 10** (freedom of expression).

The domestic UK restrictions on freedom of assembly are contained in the **Public Order Act 1986 (POA 1986)**, the key provisions of which (in relation to public protests) are set out below. It is important when applying these provisions to a problem question to consider them in the light of **Articles 10 and 11** and to discuss the **proportionality** of action taken by the police.

KEY CASE: *R (Laporte) v Chief Constable of Gloucestershire* [2006] UKHL 55

Background:

L was on one of three coaches travelling from London to join an anti-war demonstration in Gloucestershire. The police, fearing that the coaches contained members of a violent anarchist group, stopped them and forced them to return to London under police escort. L argued that this infringed her right to freedom of peaceful assembly (Article 11) and her right to freedom of expression (Article 10). C accepted that he had detained L, but argued that her detention was proportionate to prevent likely breaches of the peace.

Principle:

The House of Lords held:

- The infringement of L's rights was not prescribed by law as breach of the peace was not 'imminent' and so the police had no power to arrest or to detain L in these circumstances.
- Only 8 of the 120 passengers on the coaches were members of the anarchist group, and so it was unreasonable and disproportionate to detain all of the passengers.

It was, in any event, unreasonable of the police to believe that there would be disorder once the coaches got to the demonstration, given the extensive precautions in place there.

In *James v Director of Public Prosecutions* (2015), it was held that the proportionality of the senior police officer's decision to impose conditions on a public assembly under **s 14 POA 1986** (see below) could be raised in argument as a defence to a prosecution for failure to comply with those conditions.

POA 1986

Part 2 POA 1986 contains measures to enable the police to control most public meetings and processions. POA 1986 also provides for criminal sanctions for breach of its provisions.

Processions: advance notice

POA 1986 itself does not define 'procession', but at common law a procession has been defined as **'a body of persons moving along a route'** (*Flockhart v Robinson* (1950)) and therefore requires more than one person to be involved. The POA 1986 controls apply to processions held **'in a public place' (s 16)**.

The organisers must give the police **6 clear days'** advance written notice of a public procession in accordance with **s 11** unless it is not reasonably practicable to do so, or the procession falls within a funeral or customary procession (e.g. a Remembrance Day parade).

Processions: imposing conditions

Section 12 permits the police to **impose conditions** on a procession where they **reasonably believe** that it may result in:

- serious public disorder;
- serious property damage; or
- serious disruption to the community.

Conditions can also be imposed if the organisers' purpose is **to intimidate others**. They can be imposed in advance of the procession by the Chief Constable and, once the procession is under way, by the most senior officer on the scene. The conditions must be **proportionate**, i.e. necessary to prevent the anticipated disorder, damage, disruption or intimidation. They may, for example, include directions as to the time, date or route of the procession.

If the organisers and/or participants of the procession do not comply with lawfully imposed police conditions, they are guilty of a criminal offence – see **s 12(4)–(10)** for the various offences and penalties.

Processions: bans

There is a limited power under **s 13** for a **District Council** to ban processions in its area, where the Chief Constable so requests. Such a request may only be made where the police consider that their **s 12 power to impose conditions is inadequate to prevent serious public disorder**. A banning order requires the consent of the **Home Secretary**.

It is an offence to contravene a banning order: **see s 13(7)–(13)**.

Challenging directions and/or banning orders

POA 1986 itself contains no mechanism to challenge either the imposition of directions on a procession or a banning order. However, someone affected may:

- make a claim for judicial review;
- raise the illegality or proportionality of directions (or a banning order) as a defence to any criminal charge for alleged contravention; or
- claim against the police for damages, e.g. in the tort of false imprisonment.

KEY CASE: *Austin v Commissioner of Police of the Metropolis* [2009] UKHL 5

Background:

On May Day 2001, a crowd of demonstrators marched into Oxford Circus in London. At one point there were 3,000 people inside the Circus, with crowds of thousands assembled just outside in Oxford Street. There was some serious violence and several arrests were made. The organisers had deliberately given no advance notice of the procession and had generally refused to co-operate with the police.

Oxford Circus was cordoned off by the police. From about 2.20 pm, people could only leave with the permission of the police, and the claimants were prevented from leaving for over 7 hours. They said that their requests to be released earlier had been turned down. Both claimants issued proceedings for damages in false imprisonment and under HRA 1998 for breach of the right to liberty under Article 5.

Principle:

The House of Lords held that any steps taken to restrict an individual's liberty must be taken in good faith and must be proportionate. If those requirements were met, measures of crowd control undertaken in the interests of the community would not infringe Article 5.

Here, the intention of the police had been to maintain the cordon only so long as was reasonably thought necessary to achieve a controlled dispersal in an unusually difficult situation. The confinement and restriction of movement imposed did not therefore breach Article 5. The claim was dismissed.

Assemblies: definition

The controls in POA 1986 apply only to a 'public assembly', as defined in **s 16**, i.e.:

- an assembly of **two or more people**;
- in a **public place**;
- which is wholly or partly **open to the air.**

'Public place' includes any highway or any place to which the public have access (whether on payment or free of charge) as of right or by permission.

Private meetings (whether indoors or outdoors) do not fall within POA 1986, but can be dispersed by the police using common law powers to prevent an imminent breach of the peace.

Note also, following the High Court's decision in *R (Hicks v Commissioner of Police of the Metropolis* (2012), that the police may rely on common law powers to arrest protesters for an imminent breach of the peace where they fear that the protest is likely to lead to violence against the protesters themselves. In that case, the arrests were held to be proportionate under Articles 10 and 11 in relation to the policing of demonstrations on the day of the Royal Wedding.

Assemblies: imposing conditions

Conditions can be imposed under **s 14** on similar grounds, and for similar purposes, to those for processions. They may include, for example, conditions about the location, duration and maximum number of attendees. Again, breach of a lawfully imposed condition is a criminal offence – see **s 14(4)–(10)** for the various offences and penalties.

Trespassory assemblies

Sections 14A–14C POA 1986 contain a limited power for a council (at the request of the police and with the Home Secretary's consent) to prohibit a 'trespassory assembly', i.e. one which the Chief Officer of Police reasonably believes is on land to which the public have no right of access and for which permission has not been given by the land's occupier.

The power to request a banning order arises where the police reasonably believe that the trespassory assembly may result in:

- serious disruption to community life; or
- significant damage to land or to a building or monument of historical, archaeological or scientific importance (e.g. Stonehenge).

POA 1986: exam tips

Exam questions on POA 1986 tend to follow a similar format to PACE 1984, i.e. a problem scenario which requires you to analyse a series of events taking place in the context of a public procession or assembly (or sometimes both!) and to discuss the legality of police action – which you should consider both from a POA 1986 and a human rights perspective.

The **'DIA-GRAM'** approach recommended for PACE 1984 works well for POA 1986 questions too.

POA 1986: revision tip

A key lawyer's skill is the ability to analyse complex legal provisions and break them down into manageable chunks. The table opposite summarises the key provisions of **s 12 POA 1986**, so that you have a record of the elements which need to be present in order for the police to impose conditions on a **public procession**.

You can use this to aid your exam revision. Note the level of detail required – you need to cite not just the section, but also the relevant subsection for the appropriate police power (i.e. when advising who is entitled to impose conditions, which definition of the 'senior officer' do you apply – s 12(2)(b) or s 12(2)(a)? This will depend on the circumstances).

You may wish to prepare a similar table of your own for **s 14 POA 1986**, so that you also have a record of the elements which need to be present in order for the police to impose conditions on a **public assembly**.

Element	Requirement	Section
Who?	Senior Police Officer i.e. the Chief Officer of Police or the most senior officer on the scene.	**s 12(1)** **s 12(2)(b)** **s 12(2)(a)**
What?	Can give directions to organisers and/or participants, including conditions as to the route of the procession or barring it from any public place. Note: various offences for failure to comply.	**s 12(1)** **s 12(4)–(10)**
Why?	On the grounds that the directions are necessary to prevent any of the following: • serious disorder; • serious property damage; • serious disruption to community life; • intimidation.	**s 12(1)**
When?	When the Senior Police Officer reasonably believes that the procession may result in any of the above.	**s 12(1)**
How?	If given by the Chief Officer in advance of the procession, in writing. Otherwise, can be given 'on the spot' by the most senior police officer present.	**s 12(3)**

SUMMARY

- PACE 1984 is the main source of police powers, which must be analysed in the context of Articles 5 and 6 of the Convention.
- Domestic restrictions on the right to freedom of assembly are set out in POA 1986, which must be analysed in the context of Articles 10 and 11 of the Convention.
- Exam questions on these topics require knowledge and application of the relevant statutory provisions and case law.
- You should also consider whether the police actions are compatible with the relevant Convention rights (which requires, where Articles 10 and/or 11 are engaged, a discussion of proportionality).

FURTHER READING

Editorial, 'We need transparency in stop and search', *The Observer* (8 January 2012), available at www.guardian.co.uk/commentisfree/2012/jan/08/observer-editorial-stop-and-search-reform – this contains statistics on the relative frequency with which different ethnic groups are subjected to stop and search by the police.

O'Brien, M, *The Death of Justice: Guilty Until Proven Innocent*, 2008, Aberystwyth: Y Lolfa – an autobiographical account of Michael O'Brien's 11-year wrongful imprisonment for a murder he did not commit. An eye-opening account of serious failings made by the police and criminal justice system.

www.bbc.co.uk/news/uk-england-london-16550021 – an analysis piece featuring interviews with barristers about how Articles 10 and 11 of the Convention impacted on the Occupy London protest outside St Paul's Cathedral in late 2011.

COMPANION WEBSITE

An online glossary compiled by the author is available on the companion website: www.routledge.com/cw/beginningthelaw

Chapter 11

Preparing for your examination

LEARNING OBJECTIVES

After reading this chapter, you should be able to:

- Understand how to interpret exam questions
- Be able to formulate a plan about how you will answer them
- Know what your examiner is looking for
- Be able to develop a structured approach to revision
- Have an overview of some key contemporary issues of constitutional reform.

INTRODUCTION

It should be apparent from the preceding chapters of this book that the UK's constitution is dynamic! In particular, the last 20 years have seen an unprecedented amount of major constitutional legislation, including the Human Rights Act 1998 (HRA 1998), the Scotland Act 1998, the Government of Wales Acts 1998 and 2006, the Constitutional Reform Act 2005 and the European Union Act 2011.

The pace of change shows no sign of slowing. Even with competing political priorities such as economic crises, threats of terrorism and public services reform, successive Governments have continued to include constitutional reform on their legislative agenda.

High-profile current issues include: the Government's proposals to repeal HRA 1998; an upcoming referendum on the UK's membership of the European Union (EU); the continuing debate about the future role and composition of the House of Lords; and the future of the UK itself, as the division of power between Westminster and the devolved administrations comes under increasing strain.

In this chapter we conclude our introduction to the UK's constitution by considering how to write essays to answer questions about the areas ripest for potential change. This will not only help you to prepare for examinations in constitutional law (most examiners like to set questions of contemporary relevance, and proposed reforms are a favourite topic!), but, perhaps more importantly, will help you to consolidate your understanding of issues on which you may well, in the near future, be asked to vote.

HOW TO BE PREPARED FOR ESSAY QUESTIONS ON CONSTITUTIONAL REFORM TOPICS

It is important to know why your examiner is asking you the question! Examiners rarely ambush you – they tend to set essay questions on topics (a) which (provided you have attended regularly!) have been covered in lectures and seminars, and (b) which have some contemporary relevance, e.g. which have been in the news that academic year. It is therefore important to keep up to date with the news, and doing so will add context, depth and authority to your essays.

This does not mean that you need to read *The Times* from cover to cover each day! We all have busy working, family and social lives, and you need to find an efficient (and, preferably, enjoyable!) way to keep up to date with current affairs. As you probably gathered from Chapter 2, I am a big sports fan – so I constantly have BBC Radio 5 Live on in the car, the kitchen, etc. Amongst the updates on the continuing glories of the England cricket team (and the continuing decline of my football team, Aston Villa), there are half-hourly, 5-minute news bulletins which, at the very least, alert me to any new issues of constitutional importance, such as Government proposals for reform, which I might need to read up on.

Talk radio is not everyone's cup of tea! Other ways to keep up to date with the political news in an easily digestible, time-efficient way include:

Preferred media	Source – quick update	Source – more detail
Internet	Check a reputable website once a day, e.g. www.bbc.co.uk/news, or better still www.bbc.co.uk/news/politics. Unlike some other broadcasters, the BBC is politically independent and tends to give a balanced view of arguments for and against potential constitutional reforms.	Save to your internet favourites some websites containing more in-depth analysis of constitutional reform stories. Examples include www.guardian.co.uk/politics/constitution and www.telegraph.co.uk/news/politics. You should be aware that these two sources come from very different perspectives – The Guardian newspaper tends to support the Labour Party, while the Daily Telegraph tends to support the Conservative Party. That does not mean that it is wrong to use them, but you need to use such material critically and to be aware of any potential bias on the part of the author. For a more in-depth, legal analysis of developments in the constitution and relevant case law, see the excellent and regularly updated UK Constitutional Law Association blog: http://ukconstitutionallaw.org/blog.

(Continued)

Preferred media	Source – quick update	Source – more detail
TV	Watch BBC or ITN News once a day.	Watch (via a recording, iPlayer or Catch Up TV if more convenient!) a topical political debate show such as BBC1's Question Time or BBC2's Newsnight.
Print	Read a quality broadsheet newspaper such as *The Times, the Daily Telegraph, The Guardian or The Independent*. If, like me, you do not have time to do this every day, the Sunday versions contain a useful digest of (and comment upon) the week's most important political stories.	Follow up on the detail of proposed constitutional reforms by reading an academic journal such as *Public Law, New Law Journal or Modern Law Review*.

Good students, i.e. those who write the best essays and get the highest marks, not only demonstrate knowledge and understanding of the key primary sources relating to the topic they are writing about, but also relate that material to the wider constitutional and political picture. In order to do this effectively within the time constraints of an exam, you need to be able to plan and structure your essays.

TRANSLATING THE QUESTION

Students would be surprised to know just how much time their lecturers (and the moderators and external examiners who approve the papers!) spend agonising over the precise wording of each question. Examiners are not trying to catch you out – they choose the wording of the question very deliberately in order to trigger particular topics, or aspects of topics, and to make it clear what you are required to do.

A good place to start is by 'translating' the question. Often, exam questions on constitutional law take the form of a quotation from a politician, academic or commentator, followed by a question or instruction ('the rubric' – often written in bold) from your examiner relating to that quotation. Here are a few tips:

- Read the quotation very carefully – then stop, and read it again! Make sure that you understand what it is saying. If you don't, then (if you have a choice) consider answering another question!

- Look at the person to whom the quotation is attributed. Is there likely to be any inherent bias in their view, which you should note and comment upon in your answer? Are they, for example, a Government Minister, an opposition politician or a writer for a particular newspaper?
- Make sure that you are absolutely clear about the rubric. Your time is limited, so use it to do exactly what your examiner has asked you to do. While context is essential, and you will get more marks for relating your answer to the bigger constitutional picture, the main part of your answer should be focused on the point (e.g. the particular case, piece of legislation or proposed reform) you are asked to discuss.

Ten of the most common trigger words used by examiners in their rubric are:

Analyse	Break down a case, piece of legislation or proposed reform into its main points, exploring in detail the reasoning behind each one and relating them to the bigger picture.
Comment	Give your view on a particular topic or theory. Identify, analyse and explain alternative views, and say why you do not share them.
Compare	Examine in detail two or more authorities, identifying and commenting upon points of difference or similarity, giving your view as to the reasons for them.
Contrast	Identify, explain and give reasons for the differences between two or more authorities.
Discuss	Identify, summarise and evaluate (see below) competing arguments in relation to the relevant topic, authority or reform.
Evaluate	Weigh up the pros and cons of competing arguments (stating which you prefer and why) in relation to a particular topic.
Explain	Set out in detail the reasons behind a piece of legislation, decision or proposed reform, relating them to the wider constitutional picture.
Illustrate	Give examples to demonstrate a particular theory, concept or doctrine (e.g. case law illustrating the doctrine of Parliamentary sovereignty). Make sure to include and deal with any evidence to the contrary.
Review	Give a brief run-down of the key features or points of a particular topic, referring to relevant authorities and commenting upon them.
Summarise	Identify, and briefly explain, the key points of the topic.

STRUCTURING YOUR ANSWER

A good essay, like any coherent written work, has a beginning, a middle and an end. There can be a great temptation in exams to spend all the time that you have allocated to each question writing down everything that you have learnt about the particular topic – don't! Spend at least 5 minutes thinking about the question, working out what it is asking you to do (and why – see above) and planning your answer.

How much you write will depend upon the time available, but quality is more important than quantity! As a general rule, you may find the following suggested structure helpful:

Introduction	One or two paragraphs in which you 'set the scene' by: • translating the question (see above); • defining any key terms or doctrines (e.g. the rule of law; Parliamentary sovereignty); • setting the context, i.e. recognising the wider constitutional picture of which this topic is a part.
Main body	Review the relevant authorities/material. Depending on the question, this could include, for example: • analysing key legislative provisions (e.g. in HRA 1998); • discussing trends in case law (e.g. in relation to Parliamentary sovereignty); • evaluating proposals for change (e.g. in the House of Lords Reform Bill). It is important that this main part of your essay demonstrates that you know and understand, in detail, the key primary sources. It is equally important that you consistently relate your discussion of them back to the question and (if there is one) to the quotation on which it is based. Doing this will make your argument more coherent and will make your work flow better.
Conclusion	A final paragraph, in which you draw together and briefly summarise the main points from your essay… and give a one sentence answer to the question! This will be relatively easy to do if you have consistently referred back to the question in the main body of your essay as suggested above. For example (and this does not have to be your view!): 'While an elected House of Lords is a positive step towards a more accountable and democratic legislature, there remain unanswered questions in relation to the primacy of the House of Commons, which may be better answered through a more holistic approach to Parliamentary reform.'

MARKING YOUR WORK

Your examiners are looking for the following qualities:

Knowledge	Detailed knowledge of the key primary sources (case law, legislation and proposed reforms) and of the main arguments and political views relating to them.
Understanding	Analysis and explanation of the reasons behind the key decisions, the aims behind the relevant legislative provisions and the wider constitutional and political context in which they operate.
Lawyer skills	An ability to define what the question asks, pick the topic apart and construct a coherent and persuasive argument in relation to it. Basing your argument upon authorities and acknowledging (while explaining why you do not share) competing views will make your work persuasive.
Written communication	A clear, efficient writing style. Make your points effectively with concise sentences and regular paragraph breaks. Punctuate your work. Avoid 'flowery language' and generalisations – be specific, considered and moderate. For coursework, always leave time to proof-read your work carefully and to run a spelling/grammar checker on Word before you submit it. Ensure that your work complies with any instructions as to format (font, pitch size, line spacing, etc.).

ANSWERING PROBLEM QUESTIONS

Specific advice is given in Chapters 8 and 10 on how to answer problem questions on judicial review, police powers and public demonstrations. But the message here is essentially the same – know the key cases in detail, develop an in-depth understanding of them and use them to answer the specific question you are asked. With a problem question, that means applying the law to the given facts in detail, and reaching a reasoned and balanced conclusion as to, for example, whether the public body's decision can be quashed, the police action is unlawful or the restriction on a demonstration is disproportionate.

QUALITY, NOT QUANTITY

My experience is that students sometimes place too much emphasis on the 'knowledge' element at the expense of the other criteria. Of course, knowledge is important! Without it, there is no opportunity to demonstrate the other qualities set out above. But, for example, if you are writing an essay on Parliamentary sovereignty, it is better to understand (and be able to discuss coherently) five or six key cases in real detail than to have a superficial knowledge of 20 cases.

PLANNING YOUR REVISION

Everyone has their own way of revising – whatever works for you is good!

There are some universal suggestions:

- make time for relaxation, socialising and physical exercise;
- eat, drink and sleep healthily;
- make a plan about how you are going to approach revision and stick to it.

On the last point, be aware that question-spotting (deciding to revise only a minimum number of topics, while ignoring others) is dangerous. Even if the topics which you had chosen to revise come up, you may find that the particular question you are asked is not to your taste. Some examiners give advance guidance about which topics the paper will contain – make sure that you revise *at least* one more topic than the minimum, so that you have it in reserve.

In any event, the students who do best in constitutional law examinations tend to be those who demonstrate a holistic understanding of the subject. For example, it is difficult to write a coherent essay evaluating proposals to reform the House of Lords without a wider understanding of how Parliament as a whole operates and interacts with the Government and the judiciary.

If you are struggling to get started with your revision, consider a topic-by-topic approach, tackling each topic with the following five-point plan.

Effective revision: a five-point plan

1. Read a brief overview of the topic, e.g. the relevant chapter in this book or your lecture notes.
2. Once you have re-familiarised yourself with the key points of the topic, read some more detailed material on it to deepen your understanding of them. Further reading is suggested at the end of each chapter of this book and will no doubt have been suggested by your lecturer.

3. Answer the on-the-spot questions in this book and the self-test questions available on the accompanying website. You should also revisit the questions covered in your seminars. Even if you have done them once already, you might have developed a different perspective on them when you come to the end of your course.

4. Attempt some past examination questions. Your lecturer may make these available to you electronically and/or in the University library. They will give you an idea of the style of question (and the favourite topics!) employed by your lecturer. Most lecturers worth their salt are willing to look over students' attempts at past papers or at least to give feedback on an essay plan.

5. 'Add value' by checking in the days before the examination any recent developments relating to the topic – e.g. what stage has a reform Bill reached? What are the main political parties saying about proposed legislation? Is there a recent journal article about a key case?

The main topics which are likely to crop up in examination questions are covered in detail in the preceding chapters of this book. What follows is a brief analysis of the key points which you need to revise in relation to some contemporary issues of constitutional reform.

REPEAL OF HRA 1998?

As discussed in Chapters 6 and 9, it is the current Government's policy to repeal HRA 1998 and to replace it with a British Bill of Rights. This is an extremely important and highly topical constitutional issue, which is likely to attract your examiner's attention.

A good essay on the potential repeal of HRA 1998 might cover the following points:

- Explain the effect of HRA 1998, i.e. to 'bring rights home' by incorporating the Convention rights into domestic law. Show that you understand the practical effect of HRA 1998, i.e. that claimants no longer have to go to the Strasbourg Court to assert and enforce their Convention rights. You might briefly discuss the benefits of this from a rule of law perspective (e.g. access to justice).
- Analyse the key provisions of HRA 1998, citing case law on each, e.g.:

  s 2 – UK courts are required to take account of (but *not* to follow) decisions of the Strasbourg Court (*R v Horncastle* (2009));

  s 3 – the obligation to 'read down' (but only *where possible*) primary and secondary legislation compatibly with Convention rights (*R v A* (2001));

  s 4 – the ability to make a declaration of incompatibility in relation to primary legislation, noting that the incompatible Act remains in force until and unless amended or repealed (*A v Secretary of State for Home Department* (2004)).

- Compare and contrast the key provisions above with the equivalent provisions in the European Communities Act 1972 (ECA 1972), noting that the method by which HRA 1998 incorporates Convention rights into domestic law is weaker than that by which ECA 1972 incorporates EU law. You might discuss:

  s 2(4) ECA 1972 – the requirement that UK courts interpret and give effect to all legislation subject to EU law, which means that the courts must set aside Acts of Parliament which contravene EU law – *Factortame* (1991). Contrast the effect of a declaration of incompatibility under **s 4 HRA 1998**, which preserves the sovereignty of Parliament, and **s 3 HRA 1998**, which requires the court to interpret legislation in line with Convention rights only 'so far as it is possible to do so';

  s 3 ECA 1972 – decisions of the Court of Justice of the European Union are binding on UK courts. Contrast this with the ability of the UK courts to depart from Strasbourg Court decisions under **s 2 HRA 1998**.

- Analyse the reasons why the UK Government says it wants to repeal HRA 1998. You might refer to the ongoing controversy about, for example, prisoner voting reform, citing *Hirst v UK* (2005) and the Government's reaction to that decision. Give your own views about whether HRA 1998 currently strikes the right balance between the judiciary, the executive and the legislature, referring to the underpinning constitutional theories of the separation of powers and the rule of law.

- Discuss the legal questions that arise from repealing HRA 1998, i.e.:

  – will the UK remain a signatory to the Convention and, if so, how will that work (note – you will need to keep a close eye on what specifically the Government proposes to replace HRA 1998 with)?;

  – how will the UK Government propose to comply with equivalent obligations in the EU Charter of Fundamental Rights (note that the outcome of the referendum on EU membership will be of crucial importance here)?

  – What will be the impact of repealing HRA 1998 on devolution, particularly in Scotland? Might it re-open the debate about Scottish independence?

  – Conclude by giving your own views about whether the proposals to repeal and replace HRA 1998 are coherent, workable and sustainable.

HOUSE OF LORDS REFORM?

Reform to the House of Lords is a popular topic with examiners, and the topic has recently returned to the news as a result of the Lords blocking the Government's proposals to cut tax credits in October 2015 and the subsequent Strathclyde Review (see Chapter 5 and the 'Further resources' section below).

A good essay on possible reform to the House of Lords could be structured as follows:

- Show your examiner, in your introduction, that you know the current composition of the House of Lords and its role within Parliament as a whole – i.e. of reviewing proposed legislation and scrutinising the executive.
- Briefly trace the history of Lords reform – in particular, the **House of Lords Act 1999** and the **Constitutional Reform Act 2005**. But don't spend too much time on this section – e.g. if you are asked to write an essay on recent proposals for reform (such as in the Strathclyde Review), your main focus should be on those proposals.
- Explain the current relationship between the Commons and the Lords, in which the Commons enjoys primacy through the **Parliament Acts 1911 and 1949**. Refer to the *Jackson* (2005) case which confirmed their validity. Comment on the reasons behind Commons primacy (democratic legitimacy – you may, if you wish, take a critical view of this, using, for example, some of the material about the first past the post system in Chapter 5 of this book).
- Refer to the **Salisbury Convention**, noting that it is not legally binding. Discuss the controversy about the Lords' vote in October 2015 to delay the Government's tax credit cuts, noting that the Lords currently have the legal power to delay or veto secondary legislation, referring to the Strathclyde Review and analysing the arguments as to whether or not the Lords acted unconstitutionally. Again, Chapter 5 will help you on these points: so will the article to which you are referred in the 'Further resources' section below.
- Identify, summarise and evaluate the key issues which reform might involve. You can use the headline options in the Strathclyde Review as a guide, as well as the wider proposals in the House of Lords Reform Bill, which was introduced but ultimately abandoned during the 2010–15 Parliament (see 'Further resources'). Explain whether you think that a predominantly elected House is necessary or desirable. Discuss the mechanics of elections, appointments and non-renewable terms, commenting on their suitability.
- Consider the potential impact of such reforms on Parliament as a whole. Is it realistic and appropriate to expect the Commons to retain primacy if the House of Lords became (predominantly and proportionately) elected? How would the public feel about voting for Lords who can, ultimately, be ignored by the Commons?
- Conclude by stating your own views on House of Lords reform. Of the proposals you have studied, which ones do you agree/disagree with and why? Can you propose any alternatives? Keep up to date with the news so that you can express a view as to the current appetite for reform among the main political parties.

Further resources

Taylor, RB, 'The House of Lords and Constitutional Conventions: The Case for Legislative Reform', UK Constitutional Law Blog (16 November 2015), available at http:// ukconstitutionallaw.org – an excellent blog piece, analysing competing arguments as to whether the Lords acted unconstitutionally in voting to delay Government proposals to cut tax credits in October 2015.

http://services.parliament.uk/bills/2012–13/houseoflordsreform.html – the official Parliament home page for the previous Government's abandoned Reform Bill, setting out its history, with links to the text of the Bill and explanatory notes.

www.official-documents.gov.uk/document/cm83/8391/8391.pdf – the Government's response to the Report of the Joint Committee on the Draft House of Lords Reform Bill, which contains some useful summaries of the rationale behind each proposal.

www.bbc.co.uk/news/uk-politics-18612233 – a BBC news piece in an accessible 'Q&A' format, explaining the background to the Bill and the reasons why it was abandoned.

www.gov.uk/government/publications/strathclyde-review-secondary-legislation-and-the-primacy-of-the-house-of-commons – the Government's home page for the Strathclyde Review, containing a link to the review itself, which contains a useful executive summary of the three main options for reform put forward by Lord Strathclyde.

THE FUTURE OF THE UNITED KINGDOM?

As noted in Chapter 6, the 2014 referendum on Scottish independence resulted in the Scots voting by 55 per cent to 45 per cent to remain part of the UK. At the time of writing, the Scottish National Party (SNP) remain in government in Scotland and continue to support Scottish independence. How might developments in other aspects of the UK's constitution impact on devolution to Scotland and Wales, and the future of the UK as a whole?

Key areas to consider here are:

- The current devolution settlement. Explain that the **Scotland Act 1998** created a Scottish Parliament and Scottish Executive with broad legislative and self-governing powers. Contrast the more limited, and incremental, devolution settlement in Wales under the **Government of Wales Acts 1998 and 2006**, described by Ron Davies (former Secretary of State for Wales) as 'a process, not an event'.
- Despite the 'no' vote in the 2014 referendum, Scottish independence remains a live issue: the pro-independence SNP remain (at the time of writing) in

government in Scotland and won 56 out of the 59 Scottish seats in the 2015 UK General Election.

- Potential reforms to other aspects of the UK's constitution may act as both a political and a legal impetus for a further referendum. The SNP opposes the UK Government's plans to repeal HRA 1998, with which the Scotland Act 1998 requires the Scottish Parliament and the Scottish Executive to comply. The Scottish First Minister, Nicola Sturgeon, argues that repealing HRA 1998 would require the consent of the Scottish Parliament under the Sewel Convention, which her SNP Government would not grant. The First Minister of Wales, Carwyn Jones, has similarly opposed the repeal of HRA 1998.

- The Sewel Convention is a political rather than a legal limitation on the UK Parliament, so that by ignoring it, Parliament would not be acting illegally, but might be argued to be acting unconstitutionally. On other devolved issues, such as the Trade Union Bill, the UK Government has (to date) been prepared to proceed without the consent of the devolved legislatures. You might speculate as to how the Supreme Court would react (following *AXA* (2011)) to an attempt by the UK Parliament to legislate to fundamentally re-draw the devolution settlements without the democratically elected devolved institutions' consent.

- If the UK were to leave the EU following a referendum on membership (due in 2016), this could also prompt a further call for Scottish independence, given the apparent public desire in Scotland to continue within the EU (see 'Further resources', below).

- Scottish independence could have a domino effect on the rest of the UK's uncodified constitution. It is unclear where it would leave the legal status of the Westminster Parliament, Great Britain (created by the **Act of Union 1707**) and the UK as a whole. Full independence for Scotland would answer the famous 'West Lothian' question: why should Scottish MPs get to vote on matters affecting the rest of the UK at Westminster, while English MPs have no say on issues decided by the Scottish Parliament? Scotland would no longer be represented by Scottish MPs at Westminster. But what about England, which has no legislative body of its own? Might Scottish independence heighten demand for one? Is the new Parliamentary procedure of 'English votes for English laws' (see Chapter 5) an adequate substitute for an English legislature or a constitutional fudge?

- While there has not, to date, been a similar level of support for independence in Wales to that in Scotland, it is possible that this could change depending on what happens in Scotland. The UK Government's draft Wales Bill, published in October 2015, met with a hostile reception from the Welsh Government and from some Welsh academic and political commentators, as it was seen as an attempt to reclaim powers devolved under the Government of Wales Act 2006 (see 'Further resources'). Some are now calling for a separate Welsh jurisdiction.

- It is important to make it clear in your essay that these are not purely legal issues. In reality, if the people of Scotland ever voted for independence, it is likely and politically expedient that a way will be found to achieve it. Whether or not they do so is likely to depend on economic issues, e.g. should Scotland take full control over its considerable energy assets (oil and gas) and 'go it alone', or would this expose it to unacceptable financial risk in a volatile global economy?
- Your essay should, however, acknowledge that the delicate balance by which the union of England, Scotland, Wales and Northern Ireland is preserved may depend on the interplay between multiple current strands of potential reform to the UK constitution.

Further resources

Elliott, M, 'HRA watch: reform, repeal, replace? Could the devolved nations block repeal of the Human Rights Act and the enactment of a new Bill of Rights?', UK Constitutional Law Blog (16 May 2015), available at http://ukconstitutionallaw.org – this considers the impact of devolution, and the Sewel Convention, on proposals to repeal HRA 1998.

McHarg, A, 'What does the Union need to do to survive?', UK Constitutional Law Blog (26 September 2014), available at http://ukconstitutionallaw.org/tag/scottish-independence – a blog run by a highly respected group of constitutional experts, including academics, former judges and the legal adviser to the House of Lords Constitution Committee.

Trench, A, 'Making "reserved powers" work for Wales', Constitution Unit Blog (24 September 2015), available at http://constitution-unit.com – this identifies potential difficulties arising from the UK Government's proposal to implement a reserved powers model of devolution for Wales.

www.theguardian.com/politics/2015/oct/16/nicola-sturgeon-new-scottish-referendum-probably-unstoppable-if-uk-votes-to-leave-eu – a report from October 2015 on the Scottish First Minister's view that the UK leaving the EU would inevitably result in a further referendum on Scottish independence.

www.walesonline.co.uk/news/politics/first-minister-vows-welsh-government-10262270 – a report from October 2015 on the First Minister of Wales' opposition to the Trade Union Bill, which the Welsh Government considers (as does the Scottish Government) to relate to devolved issues, requiring the consent of the devolved legislatures.

A CODIFIED CONSTITUTION?

Examiners in this subject often ask whether the UK would be 'better off' with a codified constitution, and the question is particularly relevant in light of the potential reforms discussed above. Some of the changes discussed above (repealing HRA 1998, leaving the EU, Scottish independence) might be the kind of seismic events which would prompt a re-assessment of the need for a codified, written constitution for the UK (or those parts which remain!).

A good essay on this topic might include the following points:

- Start by showing your examiner that you understand how the UK's uncodified constitution differs from that of almost every other nation (see Chapter 2) – e.g. some of the most important rules (like choosing the Prime Minister) are not written down and have no legal force.
- Give some specific examples contrasting the UK's constitutional arrangements with those of, for example, the USA (gun laws) or Germany (shooting down passenger jets) – again, see Chapter 2 for details. You might include a short, but memorable quotation, e.g.:

> One of the slightly bizarre features of our legal system is that we have a supreme court, populated by our most senior and respected judges, which can no more tell our parliament what to do than it can decide the tactics for the England football team.
>
> Adam Wagner, UK Human Rights Blog, 26 January 2011

- Give your essay context – you might refer to the deluge of constitutional legislation (perhaps noting the definition in *Thoburn* (2002)) passed since 1997, further devolution to Scotland and Wales, or the UK Government's proposal to repeal HRA 1998 and replace it with a British Bill of Rights as evidence for the notion that it may now be appropriate at least to consider a codified constitution. You might also refer to evidence of increasing judicial constitutional activism, e.g. *Jackson* (2005), *AXA* (2011) and *Pham* (2015). Should it be left to unelected judges to define constitutional boundaries?
- Consider the potential advantages of a codified constitution. You might argue that under our current electoral arrangements (see Chapter 5), the potential for an 'elective dictatorship' in the House of Commons means that important citizens' rights (e.g. trial by jury) are vulnerable to repeal by a majority Government for whom most electors did not vote, and that the UK's defining constitutional principle of Parliamentary sovereignty is no longer fit for purpose.
- A codified constitution could entrench key civil liberties against repeal for short-term political and economic expediency (see Chapter 6). Arguably, this would promote the **rule of law** (see Chapter 4) by subjecting Parliament to

'higher laws', enforceable by the Supreme Court. It could also put an end to ill-defined conventions and prerogative powers (see Chapter 7).

- On the other hand, you might argue that a codified constitution would be profoundly undemocratic, as it would fix future Governments with a set of values approved by a snapshot of the electorate's opinion at a particular point of time. These values might become outdated and political deadlock might lead to constitutional stagnation (as, arguably, in the case of the **2nd Amendment to the USA's Constitution**). You might also reflect that the doctrine of the **separation of powers** (Chapter 4) requires each democratically elected Parliament to be able to legislate free from judicial interference.
- Which of these views you prefer and whether you perceive them as advantages or disadvantages is up to you! You may well develop your own, alternative perspective on whether a codified constitution is necessary or desirable. If so, this book will have served its purpose! Your examiner does not want to read 100 identical answers – it is refreshing to find a candidate with something novel to say.
- Always remember that, provided your opinions are based on a proper and balanced consideration of the relevant authorities, they are worth as much as your examiner's – were there to be a referendum on a codified constitution, you would get one vote each.

Further resources

A New Magna Carta?, House of Commons Political and Constitutional Reform Committee, Second Report of Session 2014–15, 3 July 2014 – pages 19–28 set out the arguments for and against a codified constitution.

Allen, G, 'Kick-starting the debate on a codified constitution for the UK', UK Constitutional Law Blog (14 August 2014), available at http://ukconstitutionallaw.org – the veteran Labour MP and Chair of the House of Commons Select Political and Constitutional Reform Committee sets out a process by which the UK might move towards a codified constitution.

Le Sueur, A, 'Imagining judges in a written UK Constitution', UK Constitutional Law Blog (14 May 2014), available at http://ukconstitutionallaw.org – this expresses scepticism over whether there is a public and political appetite for judges to have a more active constitutional review role, and is therefore an interesting counter-piece to the judicial articles below.

www.independent.co.uk/news/uk/politics/the-big-question-why-doesnt-the-uk-have-a-written-constitution-and-does-it-matter-781975.html – now over eight years old, but a good introductory piece to the debate over whether the UK should have a codified constitution and based on an interview with the (then) Justice Secretary, Jack Straw MP.

www.independent.co.uk/news/uk/politics/uk-should-consider-a-written-constitut
ion-says-top-judge-lord-neuberger-9792250.html – an article in which Lord Neuberger,
the President of the UK Supreme Court (the UK's most senior judge), explains in a
speech to the 2014 Legal Wales Conference why he thinks it is time for the UK to have
a codified constitution.

www.supremecourt.uk/docs/speech-141010.pdf – the full text of Lord Neuberger's
speech above. The Supreme Court's website is a valuable resource, as it contains
not only the full text, and summaries, of important constitutional case law, but also
speeches given by Supreme Court judges, which often discuss issues of constitutional
significance.

COMPANION WEBSITE

An online glossary compiled by the author is available on the companion website:
www.routledge.com/cw/beginningthelaw

Index